# NATURAL FAMILY PLANNING
# BLESSED OUR MARRIAGE

## Nineteen True Stories

## Fletcher Doyle

SERVANT
BOOKS

PUBLISHED BY ST. ANTHONY MESSENGER PRESS
CINCINNATI, OHIO

*Catechism of the Catholic Church* references are taken from *Catechism of the Catholic Church,* second edition (Vatican: Libreria Editrice Vaticana, 1997). Unless otherwise noted, Scripture passages have been taken from the *Revised Standard Version,* Catholic edition. Copyright 1946, 1952, 1971 by the Division of Christian Education of the National Council of Churches of Christ in the USA. Used by permission. All rights reserved.

Cover design by Candle Light Studios
Cover photo by Francisco Navarro
Book design by Phillips Robinette, O.F.M.

LIBRARY OF CONGRESS CATALOGING-IN-PUBLICATION DATA

Doyle, Fletcher, 1954-
  Natural family planning blessed our marriage : nineteen true stories / Fletcher Doyle.
      p. cm.
  Includes bibliographical references.
  ISBN 0-86716-760-2 (pbk. : alk. paper)  1.  Birth control—Religious aspects—Catholic Church. 2.  Natural family planning. 3.  Natural family planning—Case studies.  I. Title.

HQ766.3.D69 2006
613.9'434—dc22

                                    2006000176

ISBN-13 978-0-86716-760-3
ISBN-10 0-86716-760-2

Copyright ©2006 by Fletcher Doyle. All rights reserved.

Published by Servant Books, an imprint of St. Anthony Messenger Press.
28 W. Liberty St.
Cincinnati, OH 45202
www.AmericanCatholic.org

Printed in the United States of America
Printed on acid-free paper

06 07 08 09 10 5 4 3 2 1

# Dedication

This book is dedicated to my wife Tracy, whose prayer and patience have exposed me to a world of faith that is more beautiful than anything I could have imagined. It is also dedicated to our late Holy Father, John Paul II, whose clarity in teaching the Catholic faith challenged me to become a new man in Christ.

> For this is the will of God, your sanctification: that you abstain from immorality; that each one of you know how to control his own body in holiness and honor, not in the passion of lust like heathen who do not know God.
> —1 THESSALONIANS 4:3-5

# Contents

# Acknowledgments

I would like to thank several people without whom this project would not have been possible.

The Reverend Joseph Gullo guided my wife and me toward *Humanae Vitae* at a time when we were struggling with the use of contraception. Father Marty Moleski, S.J., spent three hours with me in the residence hall at Canisius College outlining all of the reasons behind the church's teaching on birth control. He has been a source of strength for many Catholic couples in the diocese of Buffalo, New York.

Natural Family Planning practitioners Jeanette Strebel, Jeanne Karnath, Beverly Sottile-Malona, R.N., NFPP, Mary Zablocki, Nancy Cinelli and Nicole Pollard recruited witness couples, ensuring the privacy of their clients. Louise Sweet from FertilityCare Center transcribed several interviews. Dr. Chad Strittmatter, M.D., R.D.M.S., F.A.C.O.G., an NFP-only OB/GYN from the Catholic Health System, provided fact-checking and expertise on health issues.

I would especially like to point out the contributions of Mrs. Sottile-Malona, who for seventeen years was the director of the Office of Natural Family Planning in the diocese of Buffalo. Without her dogged determination to pass on this unpopular teaching of the Catholic church— often at personal cost—many couples would not have experienced its graces.

# Clearing the Hurdle

Sex has become a high hurdle for many Catholics to clear in their leap of faith. The church's stances on contraception, premarital sex, celibacy, homosexuality and the ordination of women appear to have roiled the baptismal waters. When viewed through the glasses of contemporary culture, the church's position in these matters looks anachronistic. This is especially true of contraception.

Dissenters believe that birth control frees women to use their God-given gifts in the workplace and allows married couples to bond in the conjugal act without fear of pregnancy. They think the church is insensitive to the needs of contemporary couples and out of touch with the lives of the people in its pews.

The church's position on family planning is spelled out in paragraph 2370 of the *Catechism of the Catholic Church:*

> Periodic continence, that is, the methods of birth regulation based on self-observation and the use of infertile periods [Natural Family Planning], is in conformity with the objective criteria of morality.... In contrast, "every action which, whether in anticipation of the conjugal act, or in its accomplishment, or in the development of its natural consequences, proposes, whether as an end or as a means, to render procreation impossible" is intrinsically evil.[1]

A commonly quoted statistic estimates that 80 percent of all married Catholics in the United States ignore the church's teaching on artificial birth control. According to the 1995 National Survey of Family Growth, published by the National Center for Health Statistics, 34.4 percent of Catholic women or their partners have had sterilizing operations, as opposed to 40.9 percent of all people. The figure was 45.5 percent among Protestants.[2]

Meanwhile, couples practicing Natural Family Planning (NFP) to regulate family size are in a clear minority. Teresa Notare, of the Secretariat for Pro-Life Activities of the United States Conference of Catholic Bishops, cited the 1987 National Survey of Family Growth in stating that 4 percent of Catholics practiced NFP.[3] William D. Mosher, a PH.D. statistician from the National Center for Health Statistics, advised us on June 2, 2005, that 2.2 percent of all Catholics and 3.6 percent of Catholics using some form of family planning are using periodic abstinence methods.[4] NFP couples can feel like outsiders in their own church.

Contraception is rarely if ever an issue among Protestant denominations, even among those that are the most fervently evangelical and pro-life. So if birth control is not important even to people of strong faith, why is it of concern to the Catholic church?

The covenant between man and woman, where two become one flesh, is the first one spelled out in the Bible. The late Pope John Paul II called this joining of bodies in marriage "the fundamental element of human existence in the world."[5] Marriage concerns man, but it also concerns God and therefore the church.

This fundamental element started to rupture in the mid-1960s with the sexual revolution and the widespread use of birth control. Pope Paul VI predicted in his encyclical *Humanae Vitae* that contraceptive use would open a "wide and easy" road to "conjugal infidelity and the general lowering of morality."[6] This encyclical caused an uproar in the church, drawing dissenting views from highly regarded priests and theologians who urged changes to bring Catholicism more in line with the popular culture.

## Sexual "Freedom" Takes Its Toll

The work of secular social scientists proves Paul VI right. These scientists find that contraception has hurt women physically and financially, reduced the number of marriages and increased divorce and abortion. W. Bradford Wilcox, an associate professor of sociology at the University of Virginia, wrote:

> The first problem is that the accommodationist agenda is based on bad social science. When most of these intellectuals were in their prime, the best social science suggested that the ideal posture of the church to "family change," as it was euphemistically called, was one of acceptance and support. But contemporary social science on the contentious issues of our time—such as contraception, divorce, and cohabitation—suggests just the opposite conclusion. The shifts in sexual and familial behavior to which these dissenters would like the church to accommodate herself have been revealed in study after study to be social catastrophes.[7]

One of those documenting social change wrought by contraception was the demographer Dr. Robert T. Michael of the University of Chicago. He wrote that the divorce rate doubled from 1965 to 1976, increasing along a statistical line that paralleled the availability of oral contraceptives to the general population. Half of the divorces, he stated, "can be attributed to the 'unexpected nature of the contraceptive revolution'…especially in the way that it made marriages less child-centered."[8]

The divorce rate has leveled off, with nearly half of all baby boomers (46 percent) having already divorced. The rate is lower among Catholics—divorced Catholics can't marry in the church without an annulment—than it is among Protestants and the rest of the population. Catholics and Presbyterians have the lowest divorce rates among Christians, Pentecostals the highest.[9]

There is evidence that NFP can help heal marital rupture. Couples who practice NFP divorce at rates of from less than 1 percent to a maximum of 5 percent, depending on the study.[10]

You would think that, given these statistics, society might embrace NFP. After all, single mothers head up a majority of households living in poverty, and children of divorce suffer many more problems than those raised by both biological parents. Instead Western culture considers opposition to contraception a form of misogyny, a way for men to maintain control over women. Society contends that this "intrusion into the bedroom" is sanctioned by an all-male priesthood that is more interested in power than in people.

**Contraception and Abortion**

As I mentioned previously, most Catholics and Protestants give little thought to the contraceptive issue. But here are some facts to challenge anyone of any faith who is pro-life to take a second look.

Cultural anthropologist Lionel Tiger notes "the baffling historical fact that after the pill became available in the mid-1960s, the pressure for liberal abortion intensified worldwide." He finds this fact "remarkably, even profoundly counterintuitive" yet "an implacable historical reality." He observes, "Only after women could control their reproduction excellently did they need more and more safe abortions."[11]

The increase in abortions points to the fact that a lot of women are getting pregnant when they thought they were "safe." According to the Alan Guttmacher Institute, which is the research arm of Planned Parenthood, 49 percent of the 6.3 million pregnancies in the United States each year are unplanned. Half of the unplanned pregnancies are terminated by abortion. Fifty-four percent of women who had an abortion used a contraceptive method during the month they got pregnant.[12]

In 1994, 48 percent of women aged fifteen to forty-four had had at least one unplanned pregnancy in their lives. Numbers from a 1992 study show that women can expect to have 1.42 unintended pregnancies by the time they are forty-five.[13] And most of these women are contracepting!

There is also ample evidence that hormonal contraceptives can allow a child to be conceived and then aborted. The Food and Drug Administration took high-dose estrogen pills off the market in 1988 because of health issues associated with them. Using low-dose estrogen, women may occasionally release an egg, an event known as "breakthrough ovulation," and the egg might be fertilized. The egg would be unable to implant and would be sloughed off. *The 2005 Physicians' Desk Reference* confirms that the pill causes "changes in...the endometrium [the lining of the uterus] (which reduce the likelihood of implantation)," so any fertilized egg dies.[14]

## What Is Natural Family Planning (NFP)?

One factor inhibiting the practice of NFP in our society is ignorance of it. People aren't instructed in its use, either in their parishes or in their doctors' offices, and often have skewed impressions of NFP if they have heard of it at all.

This lack of knowledge naturally leads people to ask many questions. The purpose of this book is to provide answers. In it you will learn that:

- there is a firm scientific foundation for Natural Family Planning, backed by medical research;

- current methods are so accurate that they can be used reliably to postpone pregnancy or to help a couple conceive a child;

- practicing NFP can help a woman and her doctor detect the presence of medical problems;

- although NFP and birth control can both be used to prevent pregnancy, they are radically different;

- the abstinence required to avoid pregnancy can enhance rather than detract from a couple's sex life;

- NFP can be used by all women, even those with irregular cycles;

- NFP is safer than contraceptives in regulating a woman's fertility;

- the behavior required to practice NFP brings about personal change that is good for marriage;

- cooperating with God's plan for the union of man and woman increases faith and trust in our Lord;
- practicing NFP makes us live in a way that is fully pro-life.

In defining NFP it is important to say up front what it is not. It is not the rhythm method, and it is not Catholic birth control.

The rhythm method, a predictive method used in the sixties, was based on what had happened in a woman's past cycles. A woman would keep a calendar showing her previous cycles, and from that the couple would estimate her likely date of ovulation. This method worked only when a woman had cycles of about twenty-eight days that did not vary. The rhythm method's high failure rate tells us that women's reproductive cycles aren't nearly that predictable.

Modern methods of Natural Family Planning rely on observations of a woman's current cycle and not on predictions based on past cycles, so they work even for women with irregular cycles. Modern NFP is a much more accurate predictor of ovulation time and times of fertility.

Meanwhile, calling NFP "Catholic birth control" does it a disservice because NFP does much more than allow couples to avoid having babies. There is a movement to change the name of this method to Fertility Awareness in order to embrace all of its functions. NFP teaches men and women how a woman's reproductive system works. It tells us how to interpret the body's outward signs of fertility and how to keep track of them on a chart, which might explain why some people still confuse modern methods of NFP with the calendar rhythm method.

This charting can be used two ways. If a couple doesn't want to conceive, they can see the days during which the woman is not fertile and restrict intercourse to those periods. If they want to conceive, they can see the days on which the woman most likely is ovulating and plan some time together then.

## The Science of NFP [15]

NFP is based on observations of two measurable factors: cervical fluids or mucus and basal body temperature. These vary during a woman's cycle in response to hormones that regulate her fertility. There are four reproductive hormones that work in concert during the woman's cycle: follicle-stimulating hormone, estrogen, luteinizing hormone and progesterone.[16]

The first day of the woman's cycle is the start of menstruation. As menstruation begins, the amount of follicle stimulating hormone increases. This gets fifteen to twenty eggs to start maturing, each in its own follicle. These follicles produce estrogen, which builds to a threshold.

A high level of estrogen triggers a surge of luteinizing hormone, which causes the release of an egg. The follicle that releases the egg turns into a sac that we call a *corpus luteum*. This remains on the ovarian wall and produces progesterone. At this point estrogen levels drop quickly.

The progesterone prevents the release of other eggs and causes the uterine lining (or endometrium) to thicken. A fertilized egg can implant in the uterine lining and mature to a full-term baby. If the released egg is not fertilized, or if a fertilized egg does not implant, the corpus luteum disintegrates twelve to sixteen days after ovulation. At that point progesterone production and its support of the endometrium cease, and the body sheds the uterine lining in menstruation and starts a new cycle.

The cervical fluids produced in different crypts or glands of the woman's cervix during this process are hormone-sensitive. This mucus can create channels to guide sperm to the egg, or it can block sperm from making a life-producing trip.

Mucus first appears at the start of the woman's fertile period. The type needed for conception is sensitive to estrogen. It is clear and stretchy and has the look of egg white. As the estrogen builds to its peak (on the day of ovulation), the look and feel of the woman's cervical mucus changes from pasty and tacky to clear and stretchy.

The mucus that blocks conception is sensitive to progesterone. When ovulation occurs and progesterone kicks in, the look and feel of cervical mucus changes back to pasty and tacky, or the mucus disappears altogether.[17]

Progesterone also produces a rise in a woman's basal body or waking temperature. These temperatures increase from a range of 97 to 97.5 degrees prior to ovulation to a range of 97.6 to 98.6 after ovulation.[18]

A couple records mucus observations (in the Billings Ovulation Method and the Creighton Model Method) or mucus and temperature observations (in the sympto-thermal method) on a chart. Careful monitoring of these variables allows a couple to determine the woman's approximate time of ovulation.

While fertile mucus can keep sperm alive for five days, the chances of an egg being alive more than seventy-two hours after the last citing of fertile mucus or an increase in basal body temperature are practically nil. Therefore, a couple who wishes to avoid a pregnancy will avoid genital contact from the first observation of cervical mucus until the fourth night after the observation of peak conditions for ovulation. A couple who wishes to achieve a pregnancy will have intercourse during this fertile time.

NFP *does* work. Dr. Thomas W. Hilgers, who has studied the method thoroughly, wrote that "76 percent of couples who used the days of fertility became pregnant in the *very first cycle* in which those days were used. Nine out of ten were pregnant by the third cycle and 98 percent by the sixth cycle. This supports the notion that the days of fertility as defined by the Ovulation Method *are very precise*."[19]

How precise? A major study in the *American Journal of Obstetrics and Gynecology* on "over a hundred women representing more than 1,600 total cycles of sexual exposure" using the sympto-thermal method concluded that there were "no method failures whatsoever."[20] Other studies show NFP's method failure rate (that is, when the method is used perfectly) at 2 percent.[21] The method failure rate of the condom, on the other hand, is estimated at 3 percent, but the user failure rate (the rate for actual practice) is closer to 14 percent.[22]

## On to Our Stories

The advantages of NFP range far beyond the reproductive realm. My goal is to present them along with the real-life stories of couples who have experienced them. Most of these couples volunteered to tell their stories after receiving a recruiting letter from their NFP practitioner. Several were contacted after making public statements either at marriage prep programs or even on local television.

I asked these couples what benefit the practice of NFP has had in their lives. Their responses have been grouped into four categories: It has improved the reproductive and overall health of the wife; it has brought about at least one positive change in the marital relationship; it has kept the couple unified in their goals as they address the issue of family size; and it has led them on their journey of faith.

The couples interviewed for this book generally aren't concerned with entering the great sociological or ecclesiastical debates of the day, nor are they necessarily able to quote the theological reasons behind the Catholic church's stance against contraception. Some aren't even Catholic. Religion often has played a role in their decision not to use artificial birth control, but in some cases it was of little or no influence.

These couples are concerned with building or improving their lives together as they balance work, childcare, family size, intimacy and finances. The spouses are notable for the respect they have for each other, the communication between them and the sense of shared responsibility they feel for planning their families. Their common conviction is that God made their bodies and they should honor his design, not alter it. The husbands manifest a reverence for what is going on in their wives, and the wives share a feeling of empowerment as well as gratitude for the way their husbands view their bodies.

These couples share about the benefits of practicing NFP in the hope that others will see something of themselves in their witness. They hope that other couples will choose to incorporate NFP into their marriages and so share its blessings.

# IT'S HER BODY

# How NFP Is Good for a Woman's Reproductive Health

The phrase *reproductive health* has become a euphemism for contraception and abortion, but neither of those things has anything to do with a woman's health. To the contrary, hormone-based contraceptives and abortion can adversely affect a woman's health and her ability to have children. After all, the goal of contraception is to render a healthy reproductive system unable to do what it was designed to do.

Natural methods of birth regulation are the only ones a couple doesn't have to stop using in order to conceive a child. These methods work *with* a woman's natural functions instead of against them.

## A Health Monitor

One obvious health benefit that NFP offers is that the charting allows a woman to observe changes in her cycle that might signal a medical problem. Dr. Thomas W. Hilgers gave several examples in his book *The Medical Applications of Natural Family Planning*. He wrote to doctors interested in NFP:

> For example, the young couple who presents in your office with the intentions to avoid pregnancy over the next two or three years of their marriage but she exhibits limited mucus cycles would be best advised not to delay pregnancy. In other words, delaying pregnancy in a situation like that will only make the situation worse (generally speaking, these do not spontaneously resolve on their own).
>
> In addition, if you see a person with a consistently short post-Peak phase [time between signs of ovulation and onset of menses], it might be worthwhile to evaluate the production of progesterone in that particular patient and give serious consideration to *prospectively treating* that individual so that a miscarriage may actually be prevented before the woman experiences *even* her first miscarriage.[1]

Because charting of cycles can indicate a problem in reproductive health, all women of childbearing age, married or not, would do well to learn NFP. Toni Weschler, a nationally respected women's health educator, says:

> FAM (Fertility Awareness Methods) can be a vital aid to doctors and their patients in diagnosing a number of conditions, including:
>
> 1. anovulation (lack of ovulation)
> 2. late ovulation
> 3. short luteul phases (the second phase of the cycle)
> 4. infertile cervical fluid

5. hormonal imbalances (such as PCOS [Polycystic Ovary Syndrome])

6. insufficient progesterone levels and occurrence of miscarriage

They can also help diagnose gynecological problems such as

1. irregular or abnormal bleeding

2. vaginal infections

3. urinary tract infections

4. cervical anomalies

5. breast lumps

6. premenstrual syndrome

7. miscalculated date of conception[2]

Hilgers supports these statements. He adds, "The method has become a valuable aid in the assessment of gynecologic conditions. Through an understanding of these patterns of discharges the woman and her physician can achieve a better understanding of the various abnormalities which might exist."[3]

As an example, Hilgers writes, "with a follicular ovarian cyst the [Creighton Model] NFP chart will reveal a prolonged Peak-type mucus discharge and a delayed Peak day." These cysts are supported by estrogen. Hilgers treats them with natural progesterone, which interrupts the production of estrogen.[4]

Oral contraceptives, on the other hand, alter a woman's cycle in such a way that they mask irregularities in the cycle that would indicate a health problem. In cases where oral contraceptives are used to treat problems such as Polycystic Ovary Syndrome (PCOS), the pill treats the symptoms but does not cure the underlying problem.[5]

## Problems to Avoid

Well-intentioned doctors continue to debate the effects of artificial contraception on a woman's health. Among the possible health complications associated with various oral contraceptives are myocardial infarction (heart attack), thrombosis (blood clots), cerebrovascular disorders, high blood pressure, gallstones, liver tumors, loss of vision, glucose intolerance and breast cancer.[6]

The pill also impedes a woman's reproductive ability. The pill works by causing a woman's cervical mucus to thicken. Research shows that prolonged exposure to the pill can cause the crypts that produce fertile mucus to atrophy. This can keep a woman from producing fertile mucus even when she stops taking the pill. She may resume ovulating, but her thick, hostile mucus prevents sperm from reaching the egg.[7]

The difficulty is most pronounced among women who use the pill for ten or more years without giving birth. Having children rejuvenates the cervix and keeps the crypts that produce cervical mucus active. Proper medical treatment can sometimes resolve the problem.[8]

Weschler documents other difficulties related to artificial methods. Depo-Provera increases a woman's risk of breast cancer and osteoporosis. The use of Norplant requires later surgical removal of the match-stick-sized tubes under the skin of the arm. The IUD can keep the uterus inflamed, causing painful periods.[9]

Certified fertility instructor Katie Singer says that one shot of Depo-Provera before a woman is twenty-one can result in bone loss, risking an increased chance of fractures at menopause. In addition, taking Depo-Provera shots fortwo or more years before a woman is twenty-five almost triples her risk of breast cancer.[10]

Singer also cites studies that show:

- women with a history of migraine headaches who take combined oral contraceptives are two to four times more likely to suffer a stroke as women who suffer from migraines but don't use the pill;
- women over forty-five who use the pill are 144 percent more likely to get breast cancer than women who never use it;
- the pill can decrease sensitivity to smell, which can reduce a woman's sex drive.[11]

In addition Singer quotes Dr. Stephen Langer's revelation that the pill "can cause severe bodily damage in hypothyroidism."[12] Then there are the side effects such as weight gain, mood swings and headaches.[13]

All these risks push many women to refuse to use these contraceptives. Many husbands too recognize that it is not an act of love to encourage their wives to use something that may hurt them.

Natural Family Planning has none of the side effects of the pill. It can be used to help a couple get pregnant or avoid pregnancy. It can point out fertility problems rather than mask them, and it can help some couples overcome those problems. It would be irresponsible to say that NFP is a cure-all for infertility, but it can be said with assurance that it doesn't contribute in any way to it.

NFP or Fertility Awareness teaches a woman and her spouse what is going on inside her body. This has been a real benefit to many of the couples I interviewed.

# CHAPTER ONE

# We Might Never Have Had Children

*Steve and Wendy Panaro*

A doctor put Wendy Panaro on the birth control pill when she was sixteen because of her irregular periods. The doctor did no testing to try to discover the source of her problem.

"He just said, 'This will regulate your periods,' and that was it," Wendy said. "At sixteen you don't really question what they're saying too much. And I never thought too much about it except that it was helping me have a regular cycle."

By the age of twenty-two Wendy had become a nurse, and "I started questioning this and all the ramifications of what this was doing to my body. What if someday I wanted to have kids and I'd been on a pill for ten years? What was that going to do?

"I never knew why I was having irregular periods. I was underweight; was that it? Or was it the stress of going off to college?"

When she and Steve, a PH.D. research chemist, became engaged, they began talking about having kids. Steve doubted that the pill was addressing Wendy's problem medically, so she discontinued it and started looking for other family planning options. A coworker, who was also an NFP instructor, set the couple up with an NFP practitioner. They were told how NFP works, and they decided they would use it in their married life.

Wendy charted her cycles, but for almost a year she had no period. She showed her charts to her doctor, and he was able to discern the possible problem. Blood work confirmed the fact that Wendy had Polycystic Ovary Syndrome (PCOS).

The doctor put Wendy on progesterone, which gave her withdrawal bleeding but not a cycle. She was then placed on Clomid to stimulate ovulation. NFP proved invaluable now in determining when she was fertile.

"Without NFP I could never say when I would ovulate," Wendy said. "I can ovulate on Day 50 (after menses), but how would I know that unless I charted?" With the aid of their NFP knowledge, the Panaros were able to conceive. "And we found out we were having twins!"

About eight months after their son and daughter were born, Wendy and Steve asked their doctor if the pregnancy had straightened her out hormonally. He said it had not and that their chances of getting pregnant on their own were slim to none.

"We never would have gone to any other fertility treatment, any *in vitro* or anything like that," Wendy said. "It didn't go with what we believe in. We believed that if a pregnancy was meant to happen, it would happen. And sure enough, using NPF it did!"

Two weeks after being told they couldn't have children on their own, Wendy observed a day of fertility despite not having had a cycle again. She became pregnant that day.

"Using NFP, it was so easy to find our day of fertility," Wendy said. "Without NFP I don't know if we ever would have gotten pregnant."

"Wendy wasn't even on Clomid," Steve said. "Our third is our miracle child."

The biggest benefit of NFP to Steve and Wendy was that it helped them discover that she had a fertility problem before it progressed to the point where she couldn't have children. "We weren't expecting to have fertility problems," Wendy said. "We weren't even planning to have children as soon as we did, until we found out we had a problem. Then it became an issue."

"The pill masked her problem from the age of sixteen until she was twenty-four, but it didn't address it at all," her husband said.

Both Wendy and Steve feel that young women should get to know their bodies and their cycles so that fertility problems can be addressed as soon as possible. Many women, they feel, take their fertility for granted and believe it will be functioning when they are ready to have children.

"You see people go so far as to have *in vitro*," Steve said. "They go through the emotions of trying time and time again when it may not even be necessary. My sister-in-law went through a battery of tests and several treatments, and I said, 'Why don't you just go see my doctor?' She charted and became pregnant right away. The problem was as simple as not having enough cervical mucus, which a lot of doctors don't even look for. She took one teaspoon of a cough medicine, which can increase cervical mucus, and she became pregnant right away."

Sometime after the birth of their third child, Wendy started taking medication to treat her PCOS. Her cycles became normal, and the Panaros were able to take advantage of another day of fertility. They had been married seven years when their fourth child arrived in January 2004.

"NFP is great for spacing your kids," Wendy said.

"Or not spacing your kids," Steve added.

# Chapter Two

# NFP: The Best Medicine

*Dr. Gloria Zibilich*

D r. Gloria Zibilich is in family practice in a small town in northwest Pennsylvania. She grew up in the church and never left it, even while in college, but her journey to complete acceptance of its teaching on contraception has been long and has had some unexpected twists.

Dr. Zibilich did her undergraduate studies in biology and chemistry at Clark College, an all-women Catholic college in Dubuque, Iowa. She took a basic bioethics course in 1976, and one of the issues investigated was contraception. The modern methods of NFP had been brought to the United States and developed here, but her research made mention only of rhythm and not of Natural Family Planning.

"I did read at least parts of *Humane vitae* at that time, but I also read the works of several theologians who were against *Humane vitae*," she said. "So at that time in my life I concluded that *Humanae vitae* had many good things to say, but God had given us an intelligence that allows us to have dominion over our reproductive capabilities."

Dr. Zibilich was introduced to Natural Family Planning while in a family practice residency, but it was not part of her curriculum. Rather she learned about it at an engaged couples weekend she attended with her fiancé.

"It was during that weekend that I heard a presentation

by a witness couple on their use of NFP in their marriage," Dr. Zibilich said. "It came up for discussion, and several of the women said that their own physician had never offered NFP as an option to them.

"As a young physician in training, I made the choice not to be lumped in with all these other physicians who weren't offering NFP to their patients. I took a few classes in the Creighton Model Method, which uses observations of cervical mucus to determine fertility, and charted my own cycles for a few months.

"I felt that I could offer NFP as a reasonable alternative to women. However, I wasn't convinced that it was the only morally acceptable option. So over the next several years of counseling women on contraception, I offered NFP as one choice among many. And I found that women in general were not interested in NFP, when taking a pill was much easier.

"The man to whom I was engaged at that time was supportive but was not convinced that NFP was effective. We later broke up." When she did marry, she observed but did not chart her mucus signs and used a combination of barriers during her fertile time.

Dr. Ziblich and her husband moved to Smethport, Pennsylvania, in 1992, and soon she was being recruited by the directors of the NFP office for the diocese of Erie. In 1998 they directed her to the first physicians' seminar put on by the Couple to Couple League in Cincinnati.

"It was there that I found the answer that I had been seeking for some time," Dr. Zibilich said. "I had been highly suspicious of the abortifacient potential of the birth control pill, but I had not been able to find anything in the medical literature, and I was unable to get any supporting opinions from colleagues. At the physicians' seminar I became acutely aware of the abortificient potential of chemical contraceptives. Although I had not come to the conviction that contraception was morally wrong, I knew that I didn't want to participate with any agents that could be abortifacient."

She returned to her practice with the decision to no longer prescribe contraception. She began to confront women with what she had learned when they came in to renew their prescriptions for contraception. The general response was to go to another physician for contraception and return to her for other medical problems.

One problem Dr. Zibilich faced was the lack of NFP teachers in her area. The answer to that came in August 1998 when she found herself on a turbulent plane flight.

"To relieve my anxiety, I was flipping through the back of a medical journal and looking at upcoming educational seminars," she said. "I saw an ad for Na-Pro Technology in Omaha, Nebraska. It occurred to me that this could be the key educational program that I had heard about.

"I chose to audit the course on the Creighton Model program, because fully participating physicians could not be prescribing any form of contraception. At that time I was still advising patients that barrier methods were an option."

The physician course, taught by Dr. Thomas Hilgers at the Pope Paul VI Institute, was a very intense course. "I became aware that the only way I could become an effective NFP provider was to take a stand against all contraception."

To be a medical consultant without a teaching practitioner in the geographic area would be of little benefit. So

Dr. Zibilich became a full participant in both the medical consultant and practitioner courses at the Pope Paul VI Institute. She called her office and asked that all diaphragm-fitting kits, birth control pill samples and other contraceptives be removed. "I felt relieved that I had made the right decision."

She returned to her office excited to spread the word about NFP, but suffered a big letdown. The nurse practitioner who worked in the office had reported her to the hospital administration for a failure to provide an expected service: prescribing contraception. Yet "with the grace of God I have been able to successfully pursue my goal of being an NFP-only physician," Dr. Zibilich said five years after making the switch.

"The first young lady I taught was seventeen years old. She was not sexually active. She had cycle irregularities and had been on birth control pills to regulate her bleeding. I was able to get her off the birth control pills and regulate her cycles in a manner cooperative with her natural cycle."

There were other successes. One couple had been using the sympto-thermal method, but the breastfeeding wife found it very difficult to take her temperature at the same time every day. The Creighton Model System, which focuses on observations of cervical mucus in determining the fertile period, overcame that problem.

Another client was a nurse anesthetist who had undergone a tubal ligation after having several children. Her first marriage ended in divorce, and then she married a very devout Catholic. She had a tubal reversal, achieved a pregnancy and came to Dr. Zibilich to use NFP for spacing.

A seventeen-year-old came from a dysfunctional home with an alcoholic mother; she was single and sexually active. "She had irregular cycles, so I had her chart using the Creighton Model System," Dr. Zibilich said. "During the course of the follow-ups I gave her videotapes on chastity, and she embraced the idea. She came to recognize the negative aspects of the relationship she was in and broke it off. It was rewarding to know that young people will accept the challenge of chastity."

Dr. Zibilich taught a couple from Philadelphia over the phone after their introductory visit. They initially had some trouble committing to the method, so they combined it with barrier methods. But as they continued charting, they came to embrace total NFP.

"The really exciting part is that they decided a few months ago to use the method to achieve a pregnancy," Dr. Zibilich said. "Last month the husband called to say that they had achieved a pregnancy, and I was the first one to know. They hadn't even told their parents. Since I have become an NFP-only physician, my practice has changed, and I think all for the good."

Unfortunately, many younger patients are not receptive to NFP, so Dr. Zibilich sees fewer young females in their reproductive years than she did in the past. But for those who do come, especially the teenagers, Dr. Zibilich is there not to fill their prescriptions but to encourage abstinence. "It's what's best for them," she said.

"I go home at the end of the day with a much clearer conscience. Perhaps I've had a long discussion with an unmarried woman about the virtue of chastity and abstinence. And I feel that I can honestly offer information to contracepting women that they have not heard. Many are unaware of the abortifacient potential of the contraceptives and are unaware of the many serious side effects. Many do not change their contraceptive ways, but a few do."

Dr. Zibilich travels around her diocese helping give NFP presentations to marriage prep classes. She also reaches out to many who are not Catholic, including members of a nearby Mennonite community. "There is such a strong faith among those who practice NFP," she observed, "and the bonds between husband and wife and parents and children are strong too."

Dr. Zibilich also appreciates the personal benefits of NFP. "I've been using NFP in my marriage since 1998. The absence of contraception has taken away the sense that I was doing something dirty during the sexual embrace There is a renewed wholesomeness to the nuptial act."

# CHAPTER THREE

# In Sickness and in Health

*L.G. and P.G.*

This couple wishes to remain anonymous because of the very personal nature of L.G.'s illness, Crohn's Disease, also known as inflammatory bowel disease or IBD. She needs to avoid pregnancy until her condition stabilizes, and so she uses NFP, with the blessing of her husband of eight years, because it has none of the potentially fatal complications of oral contraceptives and because it helps her track flare-ups in IBD.

The gravity of L.G.'s situation became apparent during a medical emergency in the spring of 2005. "I was suffering severe headaches after a bout with a viral infection. When it didn't clear up, my primary MD referred me to a neurologist. After an MRI, the doctor came in with a serious look on his face and asked if anyone was with me because I needed to go to the hospital right away."

L.G. had a clot and hemorrhage in her brain and also had suffered a stroke. Her husband rushed her to the emergency room, where the medical team brought the clot under control.

"Since my illness affects my blood's clotting abilities when my immune system is compromised, I have to be extremely careful about what medications I take," L.G. said. "If I had been on the pill, it would have caused serious complications, such as worsening my headache and causing more clots as well as another stroke, which could have resulted in death. I am very thankful for NFP since it works with my body, and there are no chemicals involved that would interfere with my current medical treatment."

L.G. had learned about the dangers of Crohn's and the pill years earlier.

"When I was younger I was on the pill for two weeks to control bleeding due to anemia caused by Crohn's," she said. "Then I developed a deep vein thrombosis in my right leg and had to be hospitalized. I never wanted to go through that ordeal again, but in 2001 I developed another clot in the same leg, this time without hormone treatment. To make matters worse, I started to bleed internally from the IV blood thinners and had to be transfused two units."

L.G. found out that had she still been on birth control, there would have been more serious complications. There is an increased risk of clotting during active disease inflammation in some patients with IBD, and hormone therapy is never recommended. There are some uneducated doctors who don't agree and dispense it anyway.

"I really wish more OB/GYNs would suggest NFP to women with inflammatory bowel disease, since it's obvious that the pill can cause serious harm. Also, by charting it's easier to tell whether I am experiencing an onslaught of symptoms or a hormonal flare. When I don't feel well, I just look at my chart. If I have already ovulated, I know that it's not the Crohn's but a hormonal fluctuation that has started the symptoms.

"If more women with IBD used this method, they wouldn't be experiencing breakthrough bleeding or infertility and blaming it entirely on the illness, when in reality it's the birth control they are on. Most females won't admit to that because they don't want to know the truth or inquire about safer options."

NFP is the safest option for L.G. She needs to avoid pregnancy because her medications could harm an unborn child. And with so many medications already, she didn't want to take another pill because she feared drug interactions and side effects. She also knew that breakthrough ovulation was possible with the pill, which might leave a pre-born child vulnerable.

P.G. has agreed to use NFP because he doesn't want his wife or any child they might conceive to suffer complications from medication. "My husband and I love each other very much, and we'd never ask that either of us take unnecessary risks just to satisfy our own needs. NFP has had a positive result for our marriage and our relationship with God. When we are not able to be together, we do not abstain from loving each other. We use the time to share common interests, pray together, communicate and verbalize expressions of love.

"When I am sick or hospitalized, my husband sees to it that my needs come first without giving a second thought to his. This has strengthened our bond over the years.

"With NFP there are no worries about contraceptive failures, and we share equal responsibility for avoiding a pregnancy. Since we know that we can abstain for good reasons, we have come to trust each other more and avoid the risk of treating each other like objects.

"NFP does require communication and commitment, but isn't that what marriage is all about? We have gained so much by using NFP and have lost nothing."

# CHAPTER FOUR

# God Is the Real Fertility Specialist

*Don and Kimberly Smith*

Kimberly and Don Smith had been married only three months when they decided, in December 2000, to try to have a child. When Kim wasn't pregnant after eight months, they turned to her doctor for help.

Although they accompanied their efforts with prayer, Kim admits that because she had worked as a registered nurse in OB/GYN, she had more faith in medicine than trust in God. "If the medical community can't get me pregnant with all of the technology today, then how could God?" she reasoned.

Kim's gynecologist ordered blood tests, a uterine biopsy, a pelvic sonogram, a vaginal sonogram and a painful hysterosalpingogram. Don was subjected to a semen analysis, which because of the way it was obtained left him feeling humiliated. All test results came back normal. Nearly four months later the OB/GYN said that everything medically possible had been done, and the Smiths would have to see an infertility specialist.

"Hearing this was very difficult," Kim said. "We felt lost and hopeless, as if God were punishing us. I was working in foster care, and I would see children coming in whose parents neither loved nor cared about them. There were children who had been abused and neglected. And here we were ready to give a baby a loving home. It was very difficult."

Don was equally upset. "How can there be people who do not want their babies and who abort their babies because they do not want them, and here we want a baby, can provide for a baby, would love and are praying for a baby?" he wondered.

Kim and Don saw the infertility specialist on Christmas Eve 2001. He prescribed Clomid, a drug that stimulates ovulation, and ordered another uterine biopsy. He promised to have the Smiths pregnant by April, even though he had never investigated why Kim wasn't getting pregnant.

"The specialist seemed to jump right into medical treatment," Kim said. "He never checked my cycle."

The doctor also ordered Don to go through another semen analysis. Don felt that going through this whole process during the Christmas season was "disrespectful" to the Lord.

There followed more tests and more Clomid. The doctor also prescribed artificial insemination using Don's semen, stating that it would greatly increase their chances of conceiving over intercourse alone.

"The staff at the infertility center told me that the artificial insemination was 'no big deal, only a little pressure and cramping,'" Kim said. "Most women, they assured me, came in very early in the morning, had the insemination, usually without their husbands present, and then went to work.

"This did not seem right to me. Why would a woman want to undergo a very invasive procedure, with the possibility of conceiving a child, without her husband even being there? After all, the husband has a part in this too.

Were these women just going to go to work that day as if nothing had happened?"

Kim did not go to work after the insemination. She was in pain, and she wanted to remain with her husband in case they had just conceived a child.

But they didn't conceive, even through three humiliating cycles. One time Don had to deposit a sperm sample in a cup at home and mix it with a solution provided by the doctor. Then Kim had to place the cup in her bra to keep it warm as they raced to get it to the specialist's office within the hour. They lived forty-five minutes away.

Kim felt pulled between a call to do what was right versus a desire to see what medicine could do for her. She called a hospital that had recently opened a Catholic infertility unit. The secretary told her that the doctor there lived his faith and had eight children of his own.

Kim made an appointment in April 2002, though she feared that if the doctor was "so Catholic," he might be unwilling to use infertility treatments that were against the faith. She had been reading *Life-Giving Love* by Kimberly Hahn, so she was aware that some Catholic doctors would not advise or participate in such treatments. Meanwhile, she discovered that her latest fertility treatment had failed.

At her first meeting with the NFP-only doctor, Kim was disappointed to hear that to be his patient she would have to go back to square one. "He wanted me to take a common cough medicine that increases mucus, which I had already tried," Kim said. "He wanted us to start going to Natural Family Planning classes and chart for three months before I came to see him again! We had been trying to get pregnant for sixteen months, and he wanted me to start all over.

"This just crushed me. I tried to explain to him that I was a nurse, that I knew (I thought) when I ovulated by my vaginal mucus, that I had been using an ovulation monitor (which had cost us $200) and other ovulation predictors, that I had been on infertility medication with artificial insemination and still did not get pregnant. I scheduled a second appointment for three months later, but I left that doctor's office feeling confused and unsure about what to do."

When Kim arrived home, she called the infertility specialists' office to let them know that she was not pregnant. They scheduled an appointment to "discuss the next step," which turned out to be Follistim injections at about $2,000 a pop. (Follistim is the trademark name of a synthetic follicle stimulating hormone.) The doctor advised Kim of the side effects and of the high risk of multiple conceptions. He then mentioned "selective reduction."

"I had warned my husband beforehand that if the infertility specialist mentioned 'selective reduction,' it was just a glorified word for abortion," Kim said. "We told the specialist right out that if I were to get pregnant with multiple babies, we were unwilling to have a selective reduction. We asked him if he would be willing to be our doctor throughout the pregnancy under those circumstances. He said, 'Yes, of course.'"

The Smiths agreed to try one round of Follistim with artificial insemination. The shots were painful, and Kim had to make the forty-five-minute drive to the specialists' office every day for almost two weeks for tests. Don had to call and listen to a recording every evening to find out how many vials of Follistim he was to give Kim the next evening between 6:00 and 6:30.

"I had no modesty left. I was a number, plain and simple," Kim said.

Don was beginning to feel as if he were in a race with all the infertility treatments, and he was torn seeing his wife suffer emotional and physical pain.

"Our marriage and physical love had become a chore, a schedule, an undesirable job," Kim said. "I was often short-tempered, nasty and very emotional with my husband. The hormone medications did crazy, unnatural things to me."

On May 28, 2002, two days into her course of Follistim shots, the Smiths went for their initial consultation for Natural Family Planning.

"The concept and idea seemed wonderful, but at the time I was just so overwhelmed and emotional that I did not know what I was feeling. The practitioner wanted us to start charting right away. I said no, I didn't know what I wanted to do. I just knew I wanted the shots to be over. We told her we would call her back if the shots did not work.

"The time finally came when my eggs were mature from taking the Follistim. We called the infertility office to hear instructions on when Don was to administer a shot of hCG, a chemical that stimulates ovulation. The office would schedule the insemination an exact number of hours later.

"The recording instructed us to call the office because they needed to speak to us. I called, and the nurse told me that the doctor wanted to cancel my cycle because I had too many eggs! I was infuriated. I demanded to speak to the infertility specialist. He told me that since I had so many eggs and my ovaries had responded so well to the Follistim, we could just try again the next cycle with less medication. He said that he did not want to 'chance multiples' since I wouldn't agree to selective reduction!

"I asked him, 'What if my husband still administers the hCG, and we just have intercourse instead of doing the artificial insemination, so the chances of multiples are not so high?' He said, 'The chances of conception are the same with intercourse alone or with artificial insemination.' That is not what he had told us before when he was trying to convince us to do artificial insemination!

"After everything that I had just gone through, I could not believe what the doctor was recommending. Did he have any clue of the physical pain I had experienced and of the emotional roller coaster that I was on? No, nor did he care. We decided at that moment never to go back to him again.

"It was as if a weight was being lifted off me. Something about the infertility specialist and the infertility office had not felt right from the beginning. We felt everyone was just there to make money.

"My husband did give me the shot of hCG to make me ovulate that cycle of Follistim, and we had intercourse but did not get pregnant. So we called our practitioner and scheduled an NFP appointment."

The Smiths met with the practitioner on July 3, 2002, and Kim began charting the very next day. "I could feel the instant change in our marriage, the closeness that came into it."

The Smiths could also feel a surge in their faith. Kim was raised Catholic and had attended parochial schools for eight years and a Catholic college for another four, but she was uninformed about the teachings of the church regarding reproduction and marital love before reading Kimberly

Hahn's book. Don was raised Baptist but had never been baptized. He and Kim prayed together, sometimes saying a rosary.

Kim's faith in God and prayer began to override her faith in medicine. "I came across this passage from Scripture and felt as though it were speaking directly to me: 'Trust in the LORD with all your heart, and do not rely on your own insight. In all your ways acknowledge him, and he will make straight your paths. Be not wise in your own eyes' (Proverbs 3:5–7). I had not been trusting in the Lord. I had been trusting in the medical community and in modern science to solve my infertility."

Couples learning NFP are told to abstain from intercourse during their first month of charting so that a woman can be sure that any discharge observed is cervical mucus and not semen. "There were two times that month that we were not able to abstain. It felt as if it was beyond our control," Kim said. "After each time we laid our hands over my stomach and prayed to Saint Anthony of Padua, the patron saint of infertility, asking to be blessed with a child if it was God's will."

The prayers worked. The second "infertility visit" with the NFP-only doctor turned into their first prenatal visit. Kim credits the pregnancy to divine intervention.

"We are now the blessed parents of a beautiful baby, Alexandra Ida. We thank God every day for the wonderful blessing she is to us. Putting our trust in God and conforming our will to his will made so much of a difference in our outcome."

"I felt so much closer to God and to my wife when we started NFP," Don said. Both he and the baby were baptized into the Roman Catholic church when Alexandra was six weeks old. "It was a sacred event," Kim said.

"This experience has enriched our faith and knowledge of the Catholic church. My husband and I are completely open to each other and to God's will in our marriage. We are so much closer and more understanding of each other. Physical relations are so different and wonderful; God is present with us in our physical relationship."

Kim and Don decided while she was breastfeeding Alexandra that they wanted to have a second child. Breastfeeding postpones the return of ovulation after a woman gives birth, and it can also make the signs of fertility more difficult to detect. Kim said that maybe the first time she ovulated, the night of her first clear signs of fertility, their second child was conceived. Their son Kadin John was born July 11, 2005.

# CHAPTER FIVE

# The Perfect Fit for Our Healthy Lifestyle

*Michael and Christina Montone*

My husband Michael always says that he's lived a charmed life. I have too—perhaps by association. Natural Family Planning is something we stumbled upon and grew to embrace.

A deeply faithful Catholic would have the conviction to abstain from premarital sex and then be drawn to NFP once married. Then there's us: a couple seeking to live a "natural" lifestyle, attracted to NFP for its health benefits but ultimately reaping the spiritual gifts it has offered.

We were married in 1999, and nearly six years later we've been blessed with two beautiful boys, Noah and Samuel. We believe our first child, Lillien, who passed away at eleven weeks gestation, watches over us from heaven.

Michael and I met in college. We both grew up in Catholic homes and were regulars at church on Sunday, and I attended Catholic school. But neither of us can remember being told of the value of premarital abstinence. So while we both were attending Mass in college, neither of us had the conviction to wait until we were married. We had intercourse out of wedlock and also used contraception.

It was not until Michael accompanied me to an OB/GYN appointment that our eyes were opened—just a little bit—to how immoral the birth control pill is. We learned that day about the tertiary function of the pill: that women may occasionally release an egg, referred to as "breakthrough ovulation," and that egg may be fertilized. My doctor matter-of-factly told us that the fertilized egg would be unable to implant and would be sloughed off.

For Michael especially, this was a crushing realization. He immediately hoped and prayed that we'd not conceived a life that we'd unknowingly ended.

We threw away the prescription the doctor handed us, relieved to have that unethical weight lifted off our shoulders. And we were happy to make a better health choice for me. Surely, telling your body not to ovulate—the primary function of the pill—month after month and year after year, cannot be natural. I'd often wondered what science might someday reveal about the detrimental effects hormones have on women's bodies. I was eating organic vegetables, drinking hormone-free milk and using chemical-free cleaners. I knew deep down that birth control pills did not fit into my parameter of healthy living.

We moved along to using barrier methods, unromantic as they were. Our health concerns were alleviated, but the immorality of using birth control in any form still nagged, albeit quietly and infrequently.

A little nugget of hope came our way soon after college. I was thumbing through a health food magazine and came upon an article about "natural" birth control, using a calendar and basic biology to map out times of fertility. From a health perspective it was exactly what we were looking for.

I told Michael about it, and we filed the information in the back of our minds. We had no idea that this would also be the answer to the moral struggle we'd been ignoring.

Five months before our wedding we decided to seek out this natural option. My doctor pointed me in the direction of the local Catholic hospital. The connection between NFP and Catholicism piqued my curiosity. When I called, confused telephone operators transferred me to every corner of the building, until finally I reached the lone person there who could help us.

From that point on everything fell into place. We met with our NFP practitioner and were hooked instantly. This was what we'd been longing for: healthy, moral, perfect.

Two years ago we relocated and were surprised to find a parish with an NFP ministry. Imagine, a thriving ministry devoted to dispelling the myths and proclaiming the gifts of NFP! We joined immediately. And true to ministry, what we give pales in comparison to what we receive. We're meeting others who share our enthusiasm for NFP. We're discovering the theology behind the church's teachings and the truth about contraception. We're on a humbling journey that is awakening our faith and drawing us deeper. During a recent NFP meeting a pharmacist relayed that breakthrough ovulation while on birth control pills can occur about once a year. At that moment Michael and I locked eyes, sunk into our chairs and counted the number of months we'd spent on the pill. We now understand that there's a very real possibility that we conceived children and are responsible for ending their lives. This awareness has brought us to our knees in prayer and repentance.

Through NFP the Holy Spirit strengthens our convictions and inspires us to wholeheartedly welcome God's presence in our marriage. He has shaped our heartfelt sorrow over our fornication and our use of artificial contraception into the resolve to share our experience with others, so that they might be spared the mistakes we've made.

So this is our journey to NFP. Beginning with a quest to live a healthier lifestyle, we came to wish we'd made love only within the unity of marriage. We are working through the deep hurt of knowing that we may have children waiting for us in heaven, and we are basking in the tremendous joy of having two beautiful boys on earth—and hopefully more children to come!

Our home is one where we'll proudly share our witness to the gifts of Natural Family Planning. And our prayer for our children is that they wait until they are married to give themselves completely to their spouse. How marvelous that will be!

# ABSTINENCE MAKES THE HEART GROW FONDER

## How NFP Improves the Marital Relationship

A*bstinence* is the word that turns most people off to Natural Family Planning. After all, if you can't have sex when you are married, when can you have it? And might not abstinence drive a spouse into the arms of someone else?

The difficulties in abstaining for the week to ten days needed to avoid pregnancy should not be minimized, but they are minor when we consider the damage done to male-female relations since the introduction of highly effective contraception. Pope Paul VI prophetically wrote in *Humanae Vitae*, "It is...to be feared that the man, growing used to the employment of anticonceptive practices, may finally lose respect for the woman and, no longer caring for her physical and psychological equilibrium, may come to the point of considering her as a mere instrument of selfish enjoyment, and no longer as his respected and beloved companion."[1]

Cultural anthropologist Lionel Tiger, social scientist Francis Fukuyama and economist George Akerlof document a break in the union of men and women due to contraception. They say that this break can be seen in the rapid increase in divorce, in children born to single mothers and in abortions since 1965.

Fukuyama is the Bernard L. Schwartz Professor of International Political Economy at the Paul H. Nitze School of Advanced International Studies of Johns Hopkins University and a member of the President's Council on Bioethics. He is the author of *The Great Disruption: Human Nature and the Reconstitution of Social Order.* A publisher's blurb describes "the great disruption" as what happened during the shift from an industrial to an information society, when "Western societies have endured increasing levels of crime, massive changes in fertility and family structure, decreasing levels of trust, and the triumph of individualism over community."[2]

Fukuyama says that historically the family bond has been fragile, and it has been "based on an exchange of the woman's fertility for the man's resources. Prior to the Great Disruption, all Western societies had in place a complex series of formal and informal laws, rules, norms, and obligations to protect the mother-child bond by limiting the freedom of fathers to ditch one family and start another."[3]

Fukuyama goes on to say that the pill is one of two factors that caused the breakdown of these norms: "The main impact of the Pill and the sexual revolution that followed was…to alter dramatically calculations about the risks of sex and thereby to change male behavior…. Men felt liberated from norms requiring them to look after the women whom they had gotten pregnant."[4]

Lionel Tiger, in his book *The Decline of Males*, says that men took their newfound freedom and ran with it:

> In the reproductive realm, females can now control contraception and, hence, conception. The confidence that men can have about the fatherhood of offspring has been severely reduced. A brusque sign of this is that there is negligible or only minor concern by men for the contraceptive prudence of their partners. Seventy percent of men interviewed in a study of Americans asserted that women alone were responsible for contraception, not men [Jennifer Steinhauer, "Study Finds Little Male Responsibility in Birth Control," *New York Times*, May 1995]. They have evidently come to expect free, unencumbered sex, if only because that has largely been their experience…. Male indifference is surely a factor in the 40 percent of births that are unplanned, to say nothing of the pregnancies that end in abortion.[5]

Further:

> When the man is cut out of the reproductive agreement, it is difficult to overestimate the impact of hidden contraception. That is why there is such a strong association between sexual autonomy, based on female-controlled contraception, and anunexpected array of large-gauge social and economic consequences….
>
> We have to consider the dramatic effect on men of their contraceptive ignorance. It is overwhelmingly clear in nearly every sexual encounter that, unless they have been vasectomized, when men ejaculate in their partner, they have par-

ticipated in a possible pregnancy. But if only the woman has the facts about her fertility, if only she knows the possible outcomes of the episode, what happens to a man's sense...of responsibility?[6]

The purpose of sex is to create a bond between the spouses and to create new life. It is clear that when you remove the creative aspect, you remove the unitive aspect.

## Bad for Women, Bad for Men

The Catholic church, because of its opposition to birth control, has been called anti-female. George A. Akerlof, a Nobel-prize winning economist and a professor at the University of California at Berkeley, puts the lie to that contention. He shows that women have suffered with the widespread availability of contraception and abortion.

Akerlof describes the changes that the sudden availability of inexpensive contraception and abortion brought to society in the late 1960s. It caused the erosion of the understanding that premarital sexual relations resulting in pregnancy meant that the partners would marry. This caused the number of "shotgun marriages" to fall. It put traditional women, those who wanted marriage and children, at a competitive disadvantage. The priority of "choice" left them little choice but to give in to demands for sex from men who otherwise could get it from women who would use contraception or get an abortion if a pregnancy occurred.

This resulted in a jump in the number of abortions and of births to unmarried women. From 1965 to 1969 there were fewer than 100,000 estimated abortions per year, compared to an annual average of 322,000 out-of-wedlock births. From 1980 to 1984 abortions among unmarried women averaged more than 1.25 million, while out-of-wedlock births had risen to 715,000. In 1990 there were 1.2 million out-of-wedlock births out of 4.0 million total.

In 1970 contraception caused a surge in sexual activity among girls sixteen and under and all but ended the norm of abstinence until marriage. That year there were about 400,000 out-of-wedlock births out of 3.7 million total births, a marked increase from the previous five years. Contraception made getting pregnant and giving birth the choice of the mother, leaving the father the choice of marrying or not. This caused the number of children living with mothers who never married to quintuple from 1969 through 1984. Some of these would marry, but the number of children kept by mothers who had not married within three years doubled.

> Sexual activity without commitment is increasingly expected in premarital relationships, immiserizing at least some women, since their male partners do not have to assume parental responsibility in order to engage in sexual relations.... A move to this no-commitment trap is likely to reduce welfare for all women. In this example, the gains from the advent of abortion and contraception accrue totally to the men.
>
> ...Our survey confirms a decline in intimacy between sexual partners, since relations are likely to be short term, reinforcing the unwillingness to marry.... Just at the time, about 1970, that the permanent cure to poverty seemed to be on the horizon and just at the time that women had obtained the tools to control the number and the timing of their children, single motherhood and the feminization of poverty began their long and steady rise.[7]

If women have suffered economically because of contraception, men have suffered in other ways.

Akerlof elsewhere documented the fact that contraception brought about a drop in marriage for men. "Between 1968 and 1993, the fraction of men 25 to 34 who are householders living with children declined from 66 percent to 40 percent."[8]

W. Bradford Wilcox, the associate professor of sociology I quoted earlier, sums up contraception's effect on men: "[Young men] could continue to hang out with their young male friends, and were thus more vulnerable to the drinking, partying, tomcatting and worse that is associated with unsupervised groups of young men."[9]

The substance abuse and violent crimes this created—Akerlof notes that substance abuse and incarceration more than doubled from 1968 to 1998[10]—signals that "the contraceptive revolution played a key, albeit indirect, role in the dramatic increase in social pathology and poverty this country witnessed in the 1970s; it did so by fostering sexual license, poisoning the relations between men and women, and weakening the marital vow."[11]

All of this is a disaster for society. Fukuyama says:

> Family breakdown is in itself a cause of poverty.... Empirical studies have confirmed that following divorce, households with children experience substantial drops in income, regardless of the parents' predivorce socioeconomic status. This almost always works to the detriment of women: for nonpoor families, the mother and children are left with less than 50 percent of total predivorce household income, on average, while the father's income actually rises.[12]

## Good News for Families

One positive effect of NFP is that men and women acknowledge their roles and responsibilities in the creation of new life. A second positive effect is a change in the way spouses view each other and their marital relationship.

This latter effect can be difficult for joyfully married contracepting husbands and wives to fathom. Their lives seem to prove that Paul VI was off base in his predictions that contraception would harm marriage. They can be insulted with the accusation that they have held something from each other, that they haven't experienced the fullness of conjugal love.

But couples who use Natural Family Planning attest to the benefit. NFP is really a study of fertility in which a couple learns the workings of their reproductive systems. Acquiring this knowledge can bring about profound changes in the way people view their bodies and the bodies of their spouses.

This reverence toward the body seems to increase particularly among men, even those who say they have "finished their families." Many men report new feelings of awe toward their wives as they see the changes they go through every month. The man develops a sense of gratitude for the gift of fertility the woman gives him every time they make love. She in turn develops a sense of gratitude that her husband is cooperating with her fertility instead of asking her to destroy it.

In this way both come to see that every act of intercourse is a reaffirmation of their marital commitment. Their mutual trust increases. As Akerlof writes: "It seems reasonable...that the probability of a breakup is higher for couples in uncommitted relationships than for those in committed ones."[13]

Armed with the knowledge of their fertility, the husband and wife can make mutual decisions on when to make love based on their situation in life. These decisions spark a dialogue, which keeps open the lines of communication. The couple sees that not every sexual act, especially one that can result in a pregnancy that would apparently be detrimental, is an act of love.

This can bring about a change in behavior that is beneficial to marriage. Spouses become less selfish, less centered on their own sexual needs. Abstinence becomes a sacrifice made for the good of the other. These benefits are available to couples regardless of whether they are newlyweds or have been married for twenty years.

In light of all this, why should anyone expect the church to change its teaching on contraception? Why should a church, speaking in the name of a God who is love, give its blessing to something that has led to abortion, divorce, reproductive health problems for women, the feminization of poverty, the objectification of women, poorer relationships between the sexes, more children living in poverty and more men becoming socially dysfunctional?

Blessed Mother Teresa of Calcutta got to the heart of the matter when she addressed a National Prayer Breakfast, sponsored by the U.S. Senate and House of Representatives, on February 3, 1994:

> I know that couples have to plan their family and for that there is natural family planning. The way to plan the family is natural family planning, not contraception. In destroying the power of giving life, through contraception, a husband or wife is doing something to self. This turns the attention to self and so it destroys the gifts of love in him or her. In loving, the husband and wife must turn the attention to each other as happens in natural family planning, and not to self, as happens in contraception. Once that living love is destroyed by contraception, abortion follows very easily....

We cannot solve all the problems in the world, but let us never bring in the worst problem of all, and that is to destroy love. And this is what happens when we tell people to practice contraception and abortion.

The poor are very great people. They can teach us so many beautiful things. Once one of them came to thank us for teaching her natural family planning and said: "You people who have practiced chastity, you are the best people to teach us natural family planning because it is nothing more than self-control out of love for each other." And what this poor person said is very true. These poor people maybe have nothing to eat, maybe they have not a home to live in, but they can still be great people when they are spiritually rich.

When I pick up a person from the street, hungry, I give him a plate of rice, a piece of bread. But a person who is shut out, who feels unwanted, unloved, terrified, the person who has been thrown out of society—that spiritual poverty is much harder to overcome. And abortion, which often follows from contraception, brings a people to be spiritually poor, and that is the worst poverty and the most difficult to overcome.[14]

Whether a couple is using Natural Family Planning to bring new life into existence or to avoid a pregnancy through the use of periodic abstinence, there is an element of sacrifice involved. Blessed Mother Teresa described the payoff for confronting the fear of that sacrifice as part of her statement to the Cairo Conference on Population on September 9, 1994:

God has created a world big enough for all the lives He wishes to be born. It is only our hearts that are not big enough to want them and accept them.... We are too often afraid of the sacrifices we might have to make. But where there is love, there is always sacrifice. And when we love until it hurts, there is joy and peace.[15]

And where there is joy and peace, marriage and the family can thrive.

# CHAPTER SIX

# A Woman Can Feel Special!

*Drew and Erin McNichol*

Erin and Drew McNichol didn't learn about NFP until they were married about twenty-two years, were in their forties, had four boys and considered their family complete. They were raised Catholic and were aware that the church had some restrictions on contraception, but they hadn't taken the time to investigate what they were.

"I figured that within the sacrament of marriage there were no rules," Drew said.

Their minds were changed as they plunged into an exploration of their faith. They had joined a Bible study, which led to their becoming part of a Catholic faith formation group with other couples at their parish. Their deepening resolve to learn what the church teaches, plus a chance to get away for a weekend, guided them to a parish conference with Father John Corapi, a gifted preacher and catechist.

"John Corapi is the type of priest who will hit issues head-on," Drew said. "He's not afraid to speak his mind on what the church teaches, and he says it's black and white. Either you choose to accept it or you don't accept it. And he challenged us about the whole idea of chastity and sexuality in the context of a marriage."

Several days after the conference, Erin brought up the subject of Natural Family Planning and chastity in marriage.

Both she and Drew felt that they should not expand their family at the time. The conference had brought them to a point where they could learn about and accept what the church taught about birth control.

"We've been using NFP for about a year now," Erin said, "and it's added a wonderful dimension to our marriage. It's been a sacrifice and a challenge at times, but I feel that our relationship has grown and become closer and more open.

"NFP requires communication and commitment on the part of both spouses. When a woman is fertile, the couple has to decide, 'Do we abstain or open ourselves to life?' This requires an openness that lends itself to prayer, discussion and growing together as a couple. It provides a beautiful opportunity for spiritual growth in this aspect of our marriage."

The method requires the complete cooperation of both spouses and a depth of commitment to each other that recalls their wedding vows. It also involves the male's equal participation in limiting family size, something that contemporary culture has placed solely on the shoulders of females.

Drew discovered how he hadn't been living up to his end of the bargain. It started during visits to their practitioner as they were learning the method. At the end of each visit they were asked, "How open are you to getting pregnant?"

"If you used birth control, sex was more of a convenience," Drew said. "You never thought about what would happen if you got pregnant. That's what really struck me, that you are right on the edge, that you could create life at that instant. You have to be open to that. I really had to challenge myself to say, 'What would I do?' And that gave me a whole new appreciation for the creating of life and challenged me to think about that in ways I never had before.

"One of the first months we used NFP, as we were learning the method, we had a bit of a scare because we weren't sure we were charting right. In fact, we got to a point where we didn't do it right. We went back to our practitioner, and she looked at our chart and said, 'That wasn't a day that you should have used.'

"I've got to be honest that I had let Erin do the reading of the book and learning the chart and those types of things. I said, 'I'm behind you, Erin, I really am.' I would hound her at night and say, 'What's your chart look like? I want to actually see it, and let's count.' I thought I was supporting her. I didn't realize how shallow that was until we got this initial scare.

"We prayed about the situation, and it turned out the way we intended it to. But from that moment on I made sure I looked at the chart and knew what the lettering and the stickers meant. I began to understand what NFP meant, and that really brought us together."

This changed things between them, twenty-three years into a good marriage. "I think being aware of the ability to create life gave me a new appreciation for the relationship that Erin and I had," Drew said. "Now I look at Erin and see not only her body but the cycles that she's going through and what's occurring within her. NFP allows us to get more in tune with that and to work within that natural cycle."

"I think a woman has to feel very special and appreciated when a husband respects her fertility and is willing to wait until she's not fertile to have relations," Erin said.

"When a husband can understand that, it makes a woman feel valued as a person and very much loved and cherished. She is not just an object; she is his wife.

"The beautiful aspect of NFP is that it gives you opportunities for chastity within your marriage. It gives you the wonderful opportunity to find other ways to show your love and to grow in holiness in this aspect of your marriage, in a way that you never imagined. There is such wisdom in the Catholic church and her teachings. Who would ever have thought it could reach right into that part of your marriage? But if couples seek the truth that is ultimately found in Jesus Christ and his church, if they listen to its teachings in the spirit of humility and obedience, then God will open the door for his graces so they can grow in holiness and love as a couple.

"Coming to it after years of marriage made it harder for us. We had been using a type of birth control, so it had been very easy to have relations at any time. We did have to change some; that required self-discipline. But I knew from the beginning that it was the right thing to do and a worthy challenge."

"I wish that we had started it at the beginning of our marriage," Drew said, "because I can just imagine where we would be now after twenty-three years if we had incorporated it. We would be that much further in our relationship. It's never too late to start, but I'd encourage people to start NFP as soon as possible. There is no reason to procrastinate."

# CHAPTER SEVEN

# Keeping the Home Fires Burning

*Rick and Jeanne Karnath*

Jeanne and Rick Karnath have used natural methods to plan their family for all fifteen and a half years of their marriage. During that time Jeanne has been both pupil and teacher.

Jeanne's sister was an NFP practitioner, but the couple's education didn't really begin until their Engaged Encounter weekend, when the evening was devoted to the topic. At that time Rick had the stronger faith and already knew he wouldn't ask his wife to go on the pill or use some sort of barrier when they married. So they enrolled in an NFP class and began learning the method about a month before their wedding.

It's recommended that engaged couples start the learning process six months before they are married, because it takes several months of charting for a man and a woman to really learn her reproductive cycle. Complete abstinence is required in the first month so that a woman can observe her mucus discharges without the confusing presence of semen. An engaged couple waiting until marriage to consummate their union will find this easy. Intercourse may be limited for several subsequent months while the woman charts the critical period between menses and the first signs of possible ovulation. This is best done before the honeymoon.

"It was kind of difficult when we were newly married," Jeanne said. "You think you're going to get married and be able to do whatever you want, and now you're working with the cycle and you can't do whatever you want," she laughed.

The Karnaths used NFP to avoid pregnancy for about three and a half years. It then took them about six months to get pregnant. After the birth of their first child, Devin, they learned something else.

"We used a fertile day, never thinking we would achieve again so quickly, but God had other plans," Jeanne said. "When we went in for our pregnancy evaluation, our practitioner said, 'Well, you used it for fertility.' We weren't really trying for a child, but it's really, really OK, because God obviously wanted Maggie to be here and we are thrilled."

"The one thing that I take from this—speaking to the male population out there—is that NFP gives you respect," Rick said. "You really know what goes on in a woman's body. When you get involved in the method, you can understand the cycles, and you get to respect what happens in a woman's body every month."

About half a year after Maggie was born, Jeanne started taking classes to become a practitioner in the Creighton Model of NFP. She had no idea what she was getting herself into or how much it would help her.

"The whole education program is just unbelievable," Jeanne said. "I never fathomed that it would be so earth-shattering as far as challenging my faith and everything I thought I knew or thought I was or thought I thought.

When I went to college, there was a whole feminist, pro-choice mind-set. That's what they are feeding college kids, and I bought into that.

"I never really approved of abortion or thought I would have an abortion, but I did think that if a woman were to have one, then I'd rather have her do it legally. That thinking was so wrong.

"There were people in the NFP education program who had much more experience with their faith than I did. It really struck me that there are choices out there, but the first choice is to say 'No.' This was a total change from what I had learned and what I had thought all those years.

"The program was thirteen months of highly intensive training, with a supervisor who was wonderful. Afterward I found a job teaching NFP. It opened up a whole new world for me."

About a year after Maggie was born, Jeanne started noticing some irregularities in her cycle. Her doctor advised that the quickest fix would be birth control pills. "That doctor even knew I was teaching NFP, and still he offered me the pill. I reacted with, 'I don't think so.'"

Jeanne went to her NFP medical consultant for his opinion. A blood test confirmed a condition associated with infertility. This condition can be very serious, but fortunately her case was fairly mild. The doctor prescribed a progesterone therapy to use in conjunction with her charted cycles. Within a year Jeanne was pregnant again.

"Without that NFP knowledge we might have been led down a path that wasn't the right path for us, and we might have never had Sean."

Most women aren't as educated as Jeanne. "All of the choices are not being given to women. There are a lot of people out there who have no interest in committed relationships. If there is no interest in a commitment, there is not going to be an interest in NFP. These people are out for whatever they can get, and it would be difficult to sell them on NFP.

"I often speak at pre-Cana Conferences. When I explain how you have to abstain for maybe a week or a little more during your cycle, I get these blank stares from guys. Once I mention abstinence, they tune out. You have to sell the benefits of abstinence."

Rick thinks men are really missing the boat. "Take a look at the covers of women's magazines in supermarket checkout lines, and they all promise stories that will teach couples how to improve their sex lives. But NFP is the answer for us. That's what heightens the intimacy level.

"Abstaining is something that never really bothers me," he added. "I just live by the philosophy that this gift is worth waiting for."

Abstaining is already a fact of married life. There are times when difficult pregnancies, post-partum exhaustion, work separation and illness require continence. Jeanne said her NFP clients understand this, and "they truly enjoy the time they have together and learn not to take each other for granted."

The Karnaths have seen many marriages around them fall apart. "I think they learned to take each other for granted, and I would like to think we don't do that," Jeanne said. "When we see marriages breaking apart after twelve, fifteen, twenty years, we know that's not for us. We are learning to appreciate each other more, and we really look forward to those times when we can be together."

Natural Family Planning also has helped the Karnaths

in their faith life, but Jeanne doesn't focus on this benefit when speaking to groups.

"I really try to sell this as a health issue, even if people don't get the religious part of it," she said. "We see couples who are affected by infertility coming in, especially in the last couple of years. These are often couples who have married later in life, and they haven't realized that their fertility was decreasing."

One couple in five is affected by infertility. "The clock is ticking," Jeanne said. "Women need to know in their twenties that their fertility is going to decrease at thirty-five and go down even more at thirty-seven. It gets very difficult to have a first pregnancy after that.

"On referral from our medical consultant or perhaps a friend who's had success, the couple will learn NFP and start charting their cycles. After one or two cycles, we can often see what the potential problem is. Low progesterone or short post-peaks (infertile periods after ovulation) might cause miscarriage. Our medical consultant will start the woman immediately on natural progesterone therapy to extend the post-peak. Often she gets pregnant within six months.

"Couples are thrilled when this happens. We always ask when they come in for the pregnancy evaluation, 'Do you plan on using this method after the baby?' Most often it's 'Yes!' They're sold. It's awesome, the stories we've been a part of.

"There are people who have definitely given up hope. Some have been trying on their own, and they come in thinking they really have a problem. But all they really need to do is be educated. They think, 'We have sex, and we have a baby.' Well, it does not always work that way.

"There are couples whom we have not been able to help. Some sit there and sob because they haven't achieved a pregnancy and don't know if they ever will. It's heartbreaking. I hope that they find peace in whatever the outcome is.

"Often these couples are only using the time of fertility to make love; they are not having sex at any other times of the month! I always say, 'You know, you might want to get together when there is no pressure or stress and no goal of a baby. Just have a night together. Use the time of infertility; that's OK. Keep your relationship going; don't get too fertility-focused.' Having that as the only focus can really take away from the marriage and from the marital act."

NFP has helped the Karnaths keep the home fire burning. "It's really like a honeymoon all over again," Jeanne said. "It's still fun and exciting, after fifteen and a half years, to plan for our time together."

# CHAPTER EIGHT

# Better Late Than Never

*Fletcher and Tracy Doyle*

This is the testimony of the author and his wife. Fletcher is a sports journalist, and Tracy is a physical therapist. When Fletcher converted to the Catholic church, they were confronted with the church's teachings on birth control. Their journey of faith led them to Natural Family Planning. They have two children.

### He said, "When did my wife get so beautiful?"

I joined the Catholic church in March 1997. When I told my wife I was joining the church into which she was born, it brought her great joy. But this decision also brought on a period of searching.

As we devoured information about the faith, one thing we kept bumping into was the teaching on contraception. I kept averting my eyes in the hope that the issue would just go away. We had already been married for seventeen years.

My wife, who had a head start on me in matters of faith, would not look away. She spotted an advertisement in our newspaper about a grant being given to our diocesan department of Natural Family Planning. She called the office and had a wonderful conversation.

I had been in the church for almost two years when Tracy told me that she wanted to give up contraception and try NFP. Let's just say that I suffered a mild shock. I was raised in the Presbyterian church, and birth control wasn't an issue. I was still digesting confession and devotion to Mary; contraception wasn't even on my radar screen. Besides, I was forty-five years old. What if this didn't work? Could I handle another child?

We prayed about it during Lent, after which we went to our introductory session and learned the science behind Natural Family Planning. Some quick figuring in my head as to how much abstaining this would require triggered another crisis: Can I manage this?

I scheduled a meeting with a good priest to ask him why the church is against artificial methods of birth control. I went to his residence on May 18, 1999, at 7 P.M. By 10 I had a lot of answers and another crisis: How could I not follow the teachings of this church?

Driving home from that meeting, I tried to gather my thoughts. My wife would, as always, expect me to reconstruct the evening's conversation word for word. She was waiting when I arrived home, surprised that I had been gone so long. I settled in for a long discussion.

The first thing I told her was that the church had condemned contraception from its first days and that the Romans already had methods of birth control. That was enough for her; the discussion was over, and so was our use of contraception.

This change of behavior brought about others in me. NFP requires a mental discipline that I lacked. I've heard that you are what you think about, and my mind was filled with the idols of money, sex and fame. These left me empty and unsatisfied. I was blessed in all areas of my life, but often I found myself wanting more.

The things that were going through my head were sins against chastity, and chastity is required to get through the periods of abstinence required by NFP. You have to guard what you look at and what you think about.

I heard someone say that your spouse should be your banquet table. The reasoning behind this became clear. Checking out women invites comparisons to your spouse, which is grossly unfair. I concluded that the idea that you can look at the menu as long as you don't eat is false.

Chastity is not abstinence only. Rather, it is the proper ordering of the desires toward your state in life. In marriage I pledge to be faithful to my spouse, and that means in thought, word and deed.

I also should never do something that reduces the dignity of someone else. Chastity allows me to refrain from using others, spouse or stranger, as sex objects, thereby maintaining their dignity as persons made in the image and likeness of God.

This has brought about a profound change in the way I look at my wife, a woman I adored even before we heard of Natural Family Planning. She became even more beautiful to me. Now, more than ever before, I had to consider her in her entirety as a human person and avoid the trap of thinking of her as someone to take care of my needs.

In fact, when I see any beautiful woman now, I think of the benevolence of a God who brought women into the world so that men would not have to be alone. I see all women as made in the image of a God who is love, never to be used by me even in the privacy of my own mind.

My life with my wife became more an act of giving rather than taking. When we threw out the contraception, I knew she trusted me to stand by her if she got pregnant again, even if this meant I would be attending my child's high school graduation the same year I retired. Knowing this makes every act of intercourse even more special and leaves me in awe that this special woman will do this for me.

My appreciation for what I had in life increased exponentially, and I became fully aware of my blessings. This has brought me great peace. God really does know best.

Once the wall of separation between church and the state of my sex life tumbled, my faith life flourished. I began to see that the teachings of the Catholic church were beneficial and not intrusions. And so I began the ongoing process of saying yes to them.

My only regret with NFP is that I didn't learn of it sooner. Then I wouldn't have waited so long to experience the joy I now feel.

**She said, "I don't have to say one thing and live another."**
When my husband and I married in 1980, using birth control seemed perfectly logical and reasonable. I was Catholic, and my husband was not. We went through a marriage preparation course at the Catholic church, but I do not recall any instruction in methods of family planning or discussion about why the church is against birth control. My husband's church had no problems with birth control, and since I could not articulate the Catholic position, we did not give it another thought.

After seventeen years of marriage, I was shocked when my husband decided to enter the Rite of Christian Initiation of Adults (RCIA) in the Catholic church. I had never pushed him about religion. He had attended Mass with me sporadically in the first years of our marriage and more frequently once we had children.

RCIA met weekly from October until Easter, and in the last three months of instruction, sponsors were invited to attend the classes. I attended as Fletcher's sponsor, and I decided to read all the information he had been given so I could keep pace with what he was learning. As I studied, I began to learn about my faith and experience the teachings in a very personal way.

When my husband entered the church, we were still not sure about the church's stance on birth control. Our RCIA program did not address this issue very well, and we were too embarrassed to ask the questions we needed answers to.

Ultimately I talked to a priest, and he recommended that I read *Humanae Vitae*. The document was difficult to understand at first, but it got me thinking. I then sought more information about natural methods of birth regulation approved by the church.

One day I spotted a brief article in the newspaper that mentioned a state grant being offered to the Natural Family Planning Office in our diocese. I didn't even know there was such an office. I soon spoke to the director, and she told me how NFP could help me live the teachings of the church within my marriage.

I was so excited. I felt as if I could finally be completely honest with God. Now all I had to do was convince my husband.

When I told Fletcher that I wanted to start using NFP, he was speechless. It was right around Lent, and we had decided to recite a rosary together daily as our Lenten sacrifice. I suggested we ask Mary, the mother of Jesus, for guidance. So one of our petitions in our daily rosary was whether participating in NFP would be pleasing to God.

We laugh now at what Mary did with that prayer. Doors couldn't open fast enough to lead us closer to NFP. Our hearts were changed almost overnight, and my husband became an ardent NFP supporter.

I won't say that it wasn't difficult to make this change, but the blessings that have come from it are too numerous to mention. Most importantly, I felt that I was able to say yes to God completely for the first time in my life. I realized that I had not trusted God with my fertility. I had wanted him in every part of my life except the bedroom. When I finally surrendered my belief that I had control of my fertility, I was able to see God's hand in everything.

My husband and I began to appreciate life more. We came to see the dignity of all human persons in all states of life. We saw the blessing of children in a profound way—not just our children, but all children.

A special blessing was that as we welcomed NFP into our lives, our young teenage daughter was coming to terms with her own sexuality. In school her mandated health education classes were teaching things with which we did not agree. Through NFP and audiotapes like Janet Smith's "Contraception, Why Not" and Pam Stenzel's tape on chastity, we taught her about the dignity of the body and how it could not be separated from the soul. We talked about the fact that our bodies are gifts from God and that he dwells within us. We told her that a true loving relationship involves mutual self-donation and love strong enough to be willing to create a new life if that is God's will. Finally, we shared that we are all capable of self-control, despite contemporary teaching that we are not.

My daughter just finished college, and these lessons have affected her deeply. She has a firm foundation in her faith and her sexuality, and she enjoys a real sense of her-personal worth and dignity. My son is in high school, and we need to be an example for him too.

With NFP I don't have to say one thing and live another. The total surrender of my fertility to God has allowed me to surrender in other aspects of my life as well. I feel at peace with my faith and my sexuality, and I am happier than I have ever been.

# CHAPTER NINE

# Forced to Work Through
# Our Selfishness

*Richard and Kimberly Worling*

Richard and Kimberly Worling carry a distinct profile among NFP users in that they are devout Evangelicals rather than Catholic. It was the witness of a young woman with cerebral palsy, Mary Genero, that pointed Kim toward NFP even before she was married.

"She was an attorney, and I was an administrator of a home for the disabled. We met at a grant-writing seminar for the disabled," Kim said. "We ended up being house-mates. She is a beautiful Catholic girl, and I am a devout Evangelical. We had lots of discussions about our faith in God and Christ—and about marriage and sex, because we were both single."

When Kim and Rich were engaged, Mary referred them to an NFP practitioner. NFP appealed to Kim for two reasons. It was a natural method, and it would require Rich to share responsibility for having or not having children.

"I really didn't like the idea of carrying the full burden of family planning," Kim said. "I wanted a man to be responsible along with me in those decisions."

Rich was open to learning NFP but received more than he bargained for at their introductory meeting. "Our instructor kind of blew us away," Kim said. "She started with these graphs up on the wall of all the different body parts, and Rich was just sinking into his seat going, 'Oh, what am I doing?'"

Their decision to use NFP put them in some strange positions ecumenically speaking. "When our pastor asked if we had talked about family planning, we told him we were doing Natural Family Planning," Rich said. "Through the Catholic church!" Kim added. They also attended a Catholic Engaged Encounter, where they told other participants about NFP.

"We had a wonderful experience there," Kim said. "It was a very intense weekend. It was helpful to see the two or three teaching couples who were at different stages of their marriage. And then there was a priest who talked about his marriage to the church, which was wonderful to see."

"One night we had an open group discussion, and we were the token Protestants," Rich said. "We said that we were going to use Natural Family Planning, and that having a pure relationship and marriage was important to us. A bunch of the Catholics sitting with us said, 'Maybe we should think about Natural Family Planning.'"

Richard and Kim met people who were taking the pill or using other means of contraception. Kim is very outspoken, so she let them know, "You are missing the boat. You don't know what you're missing here."

The Worlings were well established in their careers and in their thirties when they married. "We were older, and we are both terrible at change," Richard said. "We had differences that made it difficult for us to live together."

There is a period through which all NFP novices pass: the time of skepticism. Kim admitted thinking early in her marriage, "Oh, this isn't going to work." But it worked beautifully despite the difficulties.

There is another period through which experienced NFP users pass: the time of overconfidence. "We had been married two and a half years, and we followed the program just fine. Then one night I said, 'Oh, I'll never get pregnant.' We were on the third night or second night post-peak, when we were supposed to be abstaining."

"I knew we were in the danger zone," Rich said, "and Kim was saying, 'No, no, no, we're not.' But we both knew pregnancy could happen."

"And, *boom*, it did!" said Kim.

Rich had an experience in his youth that made him leery of having children. But when Kim was pregnant, his views toward children and her changed. "Birth is such an underrated, taken-for-granted thing," he said. "It is absolutely beautiful."

Kim agreed. "We've seen how a child brings this family full circle. Childbirth creates a beautiful completion of the marriage act. And now we are kicking ourselves that we are so old and waited so long. We'd have about ten if we could."

They did try to add to their family but faced many of the difficulties common to older couples. It took a while for Kim to get pregnant again, and then she miscarried. Worried that she might not be able to have another child, they filled out adoption papers.

Then Kim got pregnant again. She suffered bleeding throughout the pregnancy. Twice on one vacation she visited a hospital convinced that she had lost her child, but the pregnancy continued. Their son Benjamin arrived in the summer of 2004. He was saved, the doctor said, by an over-attached placenta that took nearly an hour to deliver.

The Worlings received more from NFP than children. "Rich and I saw that there was a lot of selfishness on both of our parts in different ways," Kim said, "and it caused a lot of tension right up front. If we had been on the pill, there would have been a lot of freedom to do what we wanted when we wanted. But that restrictive behavior of having to restrain X amount of the month gets very complicated very fast. So in the past six years NFP forced us to grow up, to work through the ugly parts of our personalities and to really start to be considerate of the other person. And it was all because of the sex.

"Now we understand why the pope and the church have such a strong belief in keeping the marriage act holy and free from all other intrusions," Kim said. "Early on it forces your real self to come out in the sexual act. Natural Family Planning helped our friendship and our relationship develop as a young married couple.

"Rebecca added a new depth and beauty to us. I noticed that Rich gained a real respect and awe for what I and my body were capable of. Rebecca added a new level of love in our house. It's just been a beautiful process.

"Now we've flipped to the opposite extreme from being selfish. I like to keep my husband happy even when I'm tired. And when he sees I'm exhausted, he just goes to sleep."

"I think Natural Family Planning forced us together because I had to be in tune with Kim," said Richard. "Our marriage blossomed from there. Charting her cycles helped our relationship because I knew where she was at and she knew where I was at, and we worked through some of the selfishness."

This knowledge helped Rich anticipate Kim's moods. "When we were first married," Kim shared, "I might say, 'It's my hormones,' and he'd say, 'Hormones? Pffft. It's an excuse.' Now he'll say, 'Maybe your hormones are a little off today.'"

"I could just go for a walk instead of causing a fight over it," Rich added.

The benefits the Worlings have received from NFP have put them in another unusual ecumenical position, that of Protestants praising the pope, the church and its teachings. "My hat's off to the pope and to the Catholic church for standing firm on this issue and not crumbling to America's democratic way, that if the majority rules then we should change our theology," Kim said. "Our church is filled with Catholics who are on the pill and divorced and don't want to have to 'toe the party line.' And your church has survived a couple thousand years because they've toed the line, with all the warts and everything else.

"Natural Family Planning is a fundamental principle of the Catholic church and family that cannot be ignored. Look at what it's done for our life and our family."

# CHAPTER TEN

# Planning a Family Together

*Tom and Kathy Nuttle*

Catholics and their guilt are fodder for stand-up comics, but think how much good has come about when the two have mingled. Tom and Kathy Nuttle have felt that influence. They forced themselves to an examination of conscience by teaching pre-Cana classes after their own positive experience in marriage prep before their wedding seventeen years ago. And they continued to teach despite the fact that the first couple they sat down with had been living together for a couple of years and had a three-year-old. They felt like rookies telling veterans how to play.

The Nuttles kept teaching despite another roadblock. They were using contraception, and they were being asked to teach engaged couples about Natural Family Planning.

"We felt that we wanted, as many couples do, to control our family size and the spacing of our children," Kathy said. "Every time we made the NFP presentation to our pre-Cana couples, we would look at each other and know that there was something there. We would think, 'How can we be NFP advocates to these young couples when we ourselves don't know anything about it?'"

Tom ignored the nagging guilt with the head-in-the-sand approach. "Being raised Catholic, I always felt that there was something not right about our lifestyle," he said. "But I ignored the subject of contraception by making it

Kathy's problem, even though I knew it was my issue too. I would say, 'Kathy's dealing with that.' It bugged me at the back of my conscience, but it was easy to ignore."

"We would give the NFP information we had been given, show the video and skim the surface of it," Kathy said. "It wasn't until Tom and I started our strong faith journey that we thought we needed to find out more about it. What was interesting was that Tom brought the subject up and kept at it. 'Maybe we should think about this,' he would say. And I kept thinking to myself, 'Oh, sure. This is one more thing that is going to be my responsibility, one more thing that I am going to have to take care of.'"

The Holy Spirit won the war, and after ten years of marriage and three boys, the Nuttles enrolled in an NFP class. Their intention was to avoid pregnancy. "We were pretty sure that *we* were going to stop at three children," Kathy said. "That was it. As we got more into the teaching of the church, our attitude changed."

The Nuttles decided to leave the size of their family in God's hands. They continued charting but stopped trying to avoid pregnancy. And Kathy did get pregnant.

"I miscarried, but the pregnancy gave us a renewed spark. Just the thought of having another one was a great feeling. It didn't work out, but that too is God's plan."

Tom immediately saw how NFP improved communication with his wife and made his conjugal life more self-giving. "I was no longer looking at Kathy as an object for my own pleasure," he said. "NFP made our union different, more of a total giving. That's a common way to describe it, but it's true. Because we're open to life, we're giving everything."

Tom could now preach what he was practicing. "It's not

an easy thing to stand up in front of a bunch of young couples and talk about this, but I felt that I was called to do it," he said. "It's the most important thing to talk about. All this nonsense about who's going to take out the garbage; that's real cute, but how are you going to live your life? What's it all going to be about? What's the center of it? How are you going to look at these divorce numbers and what the pill does? What kind of statement is that making in how you are starting out your life together?

"I think the statistics showing the low divorce rate among NFP users are compelling. I think this approach to how you deal with your fertility as a couple carries on to how you approach other things. It lets you take a deep breath and get back to what's important.

"It's tough being a Christian. It says right in the Bible that it's going to be a tough road if you're going to follow Jesus (see Matthew 7:14). Yet practicing NFP and teaching it to others meant real freedom for my conscience. I can go to church and say, 'I believe all of the church teachings and strive to follow them.'"

"Natural Family Planning's greatest gifts to me have been the appreciation of our fertility, the gift of life and the children that we have," Kathy said. "Even at the age we are now, we are open to life at all times.

"NFP strengthened our relationship and helped us grow stronger and closer in our faith. We just knew we were doing the right thing.

"On Catholic radio the other day a woman said that she mourns the children she could have had those years she was on birth control. That hit me really hard. I wish we had felt this way seventeen years ago. I wish we had known about NFP. It would have been the thing to do at the start of our marriage. It would have been great."

Kathy was in her early forties when she miscarried. She and Tom came to the conclusion that "if it happens it happens," but they didn't think it was going to. They gave away the maternity clothes.

You can guess what happened next. Early in 2005, her period a few weeks late, Kathy bought a home pregnancy kit. Sneaking out of bed early, she took the test and discovered she was to be a mother again at forty-four. Kathy would have to get the "hand-me-around" maternity clothes from her sister-in-law, who had just had a baby.

"I woke Tom up and said, 'You're not going to believe this.'"

"We weren't necessarily hoping and praying for a child, but we were open to it," Tom said about two months before his wife gave birth to Andrew Thomas in August 2005. "We were both shocked. We waited several months to tell the boys. I was very pleased to see our oldest son, who's sixteen, smiling ear to ear."

# CHAPTER ELEVEN

# A Family Reconnected

*Dominic and Kathy Cavaretta*

Life looked good for Dominic and Kathy Cavaretta in 1992. They had been married since 1974, had two teenage daughters and lived in a three-bedroom house. Dominic had a good job and was starting to look forward to the day when he could relax a bit.

Their next step was to become what they call "converts from birth control" and have another baby. They took that step, and they were still seeing graces as they celebrated their thirtieth wedding anniversary.

"Dominic Jr. is fifteen years younger than our youngest daughter. It's kind of crazy how he came about," Dom Sr. said in an interview in 2003.

In the early nineties Kathy was laid up for a while with a bad back, and she had a lot of time to think and to search her soul. One thing that was eating at her was the couple's use of birth control.

Then a friend invited Kathy into her home and put an NFP chart in front of her. Kathy showed it to her husband, and they had the same reaction: terror. Neither of them wanted another child—Dom was quite firm in his conviction—and they were sure that's what NFP would lead to.

"I said to the Blessed Mother, 'This is rhythm. What are you doing to me?'" Kathy said. "Everybody who uses birth control becomes dependent on it, and to think of stepping off the edge of the cliff and not using it is terrifying.

"We didn't know what was happening. So we went to see a priest friend of ours, a dear friend, who listened to our story, our fears." That led to a meeting with a practitioner, who put them at ease about the effectiveness of NFP. This woman became a good friend while teaching them NFP. The couple began to use the Creighton Model Method.

"Dom took a leap of faith without looking back," Kathy said. "He willingly used NFP and trusted in it.

"Learning the method started to bring us closer together immediately. It forced Dom and me to confront and communicate on the issues of children and family. It drew us closer together; we felt the grace immediately.

"After using the method for about a year, my fear of getting pregnant started to leave. I can't even put my finger on what the fear was. It didn't have anything to do with money, because neither of us is materialistic. We enjoy our home and our family; that's the joy of our lives. But whatever the fear was, it started to leave. I came to a new mind-set and started to desire another child."

"I didn't know what was coming over Kathy," Dom said. "I thought she was losing her mind when one night in 1992, after eighteen years of marriage, she asked me how I felt about having another child. I was in my early forties and looking along the lines of retirement.

"It was one of those times when you go to bed and she wants to talk and lays a bomb on you. I had to say, 'Let's sleep on this and talk about it some other time.' It surfaced a couple more times. I couldn't convince her to forget about it. It kept resurfacing in her mind. And she seemed to have solutions for all the reasons why I thought another child was impractical."

One issue was their home. They had a modest three-bedroom house, and each teenage daughter had her own bedroom. An addition would cost more than they had.

Then Dom remembered an insurance policy that a friend had bugged him into buying. He had signed for the policy in his mother's house as he dressed for his wedding. "I had this thing for twenty years, and it was worth some money," Dom said.

They developed a plan for an addition of a couple hundred square feet. It was a master bedroom and bathroom for Kathy and Dom and a third bedroom for the baby.

Yes, by this time Kathy was pregnant. When she passed her first trimester, Dom figured it was time to get serious, so he told her, "You just worry about having this baby, and I'll have this addition done."

"I worked night and day with the help of Saint Joseph and a few other friends I made along the way. Eighteen weeks to the day from when we broke ground, Kathy and I moved into our new bedroom. Eight or nine days later she had the baby. Say what you want, but it was the work of the Holy Spirit. It was meant to be, and it happened."

"Dom took the leap of faith, and God threw the life preserver after that," Kathy said.

The birth of Dominic Jr. paid an unexpected bonus for the Cavarettas: It brought back their daughters.

"Raising teenage daughters in the early nineties was difficult, and our family was growing apart," Dom revealed. "Our daughters wanted to do their own thing, to go here and go there and do what their friends were doing.

"When we decided to go ahead and get pregnant, we didn't know what the girls were going to think. They were thrilled, and they couldn't wait for the delivery. They were with us in the hospital when Dominic was born. I'll never forget that as long as I live. Here are my two daughters and me with my wife, who's having a baby."

This bedside gathering brought about a family reunion of sorts. "From the moment Dominic was born on August 11, 1995, you could feel something happening, just pulling our family back together," Dom said. "Our daughters started staying home more often to be with the family, to be with the baby. We started saying the rosary as a family. Try getting two teenage girls to do that. By the time Dominic could walk and talk, *he* was reciting the rosary."

"The grace extended into other areas of our life, in our faith," Kathy said. "I believe that trusting in God and being careful of the use of our fertility was the thing that we needed.

"Dom and I have always gone to Mass, and we have never stopped practicing our faith. I know that God was faithful to us because of that. He knew that we were trying. Once we got through that obstacle of the birth control, once we let go of that, the floodgates of grace opened in our marriage and our home.

"I know it has extended to our older children. Our oldest daughter and her husband have given us a beautiful grandchild already, and another one is on the way."

"The key there is 'she and her husband,'" added Dom. "One of my biggest concerns as a father was that the girls do things the right way. I couldn't be prouder of my two daughters. Our older daughter married a wonderful non-Catholic man."

"He practices NFP to support our daughter in her faith. Even a lot of Catholic guys will not do that for their wives," Kathy said.

Dom and Kathy decided that their young son needed a playmate. She conceived again but miscarried. So Dom bought roller blades for himself and his young son. They moved on to pickup ice hockey games with other families on Saturday mornings. Kathy told her husband that this son would either make them young or make them old. At age fifty-two Dom joined a hockey league of his own.

When father and son started going to Buffalo Sabres games together, Dominic proved that all those rosaries his sisters and his parents said over him were put to a good purpose. "On the way home he'd sit in the back seat, an eight-year-old, and say, 'Dad, do you want to say the rosary now?'

"Had we not made the change to NFP, I don't think any of this would have happened. Once we did the NFP thing, everything fell into order. I'm convinced that's what started it."

"I agree," his wife said. "A flow of grace started there."

"It was difficult to realize the ramifications of our use of birth control. Our whole family would have been different had we learned of this sooner. We would have had more children."

"We would have needed more than one addition on the house," her husband added.

# STAYING ON COURSE

# How NFP Keeps Spouses From Growing Apart

What do you call a couple who practices NFP?

Parents.

This joke ignores the basic fact that all married couples are potential parents each time they make love. All couples must face the question of children.

Lionel Tiger, the cultural anthropologist I quoted earlier, says that couples today are facing the question of children under much different circumstances than in the days before effective contraception. For one thing, our world has changed economically. Since 1979 women's pay has increased and is now approaching men's pay, which has decreased.[1]

Amelia Warren Tyagi, who coauthored with Elizabeth Warren *The Two-Income Trap: Why Middle-Class Mothers and Fathers Are Going Broke* (Basic, 2003), wrote in a viewpoint piece in *Time* magazine that competition for homes in the best school districts has driven up prices and left many young parents house-poor and headed toward bankruptcy.

> Over the past generation, home prices have risen twice as fast for couples with young children as for those without kids. Why? Confidence in the public schools has dwindled, leaving millions of families to conclude that the only way to ensure Junior a slot in a safe, quality school is to snatch up a home in a good school district.... Since the mid-'70s, the amount of the average family budget earmarked for the mortgage has increased a whopping 69% (adjusted for inflation). At the same time, the average father's income has increased less than 1%.[2]

There has also been a change in what our increasingly wealthy society needs for an "acceptable life."[3] Consider the cost of cell phones, high speed Internet connections, iPods and cable TV when compared to free TV, AM radios and books. Add to this the desire for luxury cars, large houses and dream vacations. In December 2003, *Newsweek* reported a trend among couples of buying new cars for dates and other formal circumstances, so that in some households there are more cars than drivers.[4]

The demands of this elevated lifestyle make it harder for a man to support a family, thus putting pressure on women to work. And with divorce common, women leap into the workforce because they know they might have to support themselves and their children in the future. In 1992 two-thirds of women with children under five were in the workforce.[5]

Women have rightly embraced the rewards of work and made important contributions in fields closed to them prior to 1960. They have taken to our universities, where in

74

2000 they outnumbered men in undergraduate and graduate programs. Women represented 57.4 percent of all students seeking bachelor's degrees in 2004, up from 42 percent in 1970.[6]

While there is much that is positive in these developments, couples should heed a word of caution. With the pill and the IUD changing what Tiger calls "the pattern of sexual interdependence" and with good jobs breaking the pattern of economic interdependence, it becomes easy for spouses to pursue individual agendas and drift apart. "It is impossible to overestimate the impact of the contraceptive pill on human arrangements," Tiger wrote.[7]

Pope John Paul II recognized the plusses and minuses for modern families in his encyclical *Familiaris Consortio*, "The Role of the Christian Family in the Modern World":

> On the one hand, in fact, there is a more lively awareness of personal freedom and greater attention to the quality of interpersonal relationships in marriage, to promoting the dignity of women, to responsible procreation, to the education of children. There is also an awareness of the need for the development of interfamily relationships, for reciprocal spiritual and material assistance, the rediscovery of the ecclesial mission proper to the family and its responsibility for the building of a more just society. On the other hand, however, signs are not lacking of a disturbing degradation of some fundamental values: a mistaken theoretical and practical concept of the independence of the spouses in relation to each other; serious misconceptions regarding the relationship of authority between parents and children; the concrete difficulties that the family itself experiences in the transmission of values; the growing number of divorces; the scourge of abortion; the ever more frequent recourse to sterilization; the appearance of a truly contraceptive mentality.[8]

Fukuyama points out that "the tendency of contemporary liberal democracies to fall prey to excessive individualism is perhaps their greatest long-term vulnerability, and is particularly visible in the most individualistic of all democracies, the United States."[9]

Female-only birth control begets individualism, according to Tiger.

> The relations between males and females have changed and ramified in complicated ways, in large measure because through effective contraception—for the first time in natural history—one sex can control the reproductive process. The result is a profound and probably enduring alteration of family patterns.[10]
>
> With the condom, once the most employed contraceptive, there was always a conscious or tacit collaboration between men and women. But with the pill that is no longer true.[11]

And of abortion Tiger wrote, "The drama of abortion arises from ancient reproductive strategies gone awry amid new technology and the novel conditions posed by an economic society founded on individuals, not families."[12]

## Two Become One

If the pill and abortion are supportive of individualism and not the family, Natural Family Planning is just the opposite. Each month couples practicing NFP find they are forced to confront what their goals are as a couple and to reevaluate why they do or don't want another child at that time. The *Catechism of the Catholic Church* tells us that we should create life responsibly but that it is the couple's "duty to make certain that their desire [to regulate births] is not motivated by selfishness" (*CCC*, #2368).

There are many good reasons why two people may not wish to expand their family. Circumstances of our lives can change, altering our plans and even our attitudes. There is job loss and illness to contend with. Some may find parenthood an unexpected joy and become more generous toward life. Others who initially want large families may find that the needs of their children would not be served well by the arrival of another one.

Reviewing these reasons, making sure they promote the good of the family and not just the individual, keeps the lines of communication open between a husband and a wife.

Natural Family Planning can be used to prevent pregnancy, but it does so in a way that does not threaten the unity of the couple. This is one of the primary ways in which Natural Family Planning differs greatly from contraception, even though both may have the same goal. We must use moral methods to achieve our goals even if our motives are pure. The *Catechism* says, "When it is a question of harmonizing married love with the responsible transmission of life, the morality of the behavior does not depend on sincere intention and evaluation of motives alone" (*CCC*, #2368).[13]

A woman will not necessarily have a lot of children if her husband acts in accordance with her fertility. As the following witnesses attest, Natural Family Planning frees a couple to decide how many children they can responsibly support while keeping them on the same page. This can keep them together as husband and wife, which ultimately is better for both of them.

# CHAPTER TWELVE

# It's Not Always Easy

*Mark and Colleen*

Colleen and Mark have always wanted to live their Catholic faith. They lived it when they were young, when failure to do so would have brought on the wrath of their parents. They lived it through high school, when they saw that failure to do so left some girls paying a big price. They lived it after meeting each other at St. Bonaventure University, saving themselves for their honeymoon, which came after they graduated. And they have lived it in their marriage, even though doing so has given them a cross.

Colleen actually owes her life to Catholic teaching. She is the last of seven children, and her mother was told to stop having kids when she lost her third child. Her parents' only allowable means of pregnancy spacing was the rhythm method.

When Colleen and Mark married, the use of contraception was out of the question. They were going to use NFP or nothing at all.

"My sister, who has three children, gave me a book on the natural method she had practiced," Colleen said. "She's ten years older than I, and that method required a lot in terms of internal observations. The method was not very scientific, and I did not understand it at all. I chose not to do it, so I got pregnant on my honeymoon."

Despite the quick arrival of their first child, they

weren't moved to space the births of subsequent children. "I called our method Russian roulette because we wanted kids, so it didn't matter at all to us," Colleen said. "And we actually used Natural Family Planning to help us achieve our second and third pregnancies. We were going for the opposite reason then."

A new house, a fourth pregnancy and the emotional needs of their children forced them to change their thinking on having more children. "We moved here four and a half years ago when our third child was a baby," Colleen said. "We put on an addition, doing a lot of the work ourselves. The day the contractors finished the shell, we became pregnant with our fourth. We looked at each other and thought, 'We just can't do this anymore.' After our fourth son was born, we started practicing NFP to avoid a pregnancy.

"People ask, 'After four boys, don't you want a girl?' And I say, 'We think we have all we can handle right now.'"

One child has an aversion to food additives, and he suffers from night terrors. A change in his diet has brought positive results, yet he cannot be overtired, overstimulated or overstressed. Colleen and Mark have established a regimen for him, which they follow consistently. Another child is severely allergic to peanuts and carries an Epi-pen.

The challenge in their practice of NFP is that Colleen's cycle is very short and shows signs of fertility nearly throughout. This means they have to abstain much more than the average couple to avoid a pregnancy.

"We say we're part of the 'yellow stamp club,'" Colleen said. Yellow stickers are used to chart the presence of mucus, which is a biomarker for fertility, after signs that ovulation has occurred. Green is used to chart days when they can be 99 percent sure Colleen is not fertile. She has many cycles with no green stamps at all.

"I wish I could have a green section here and there. Hopefully in the future I will. Mark may be unhappy with the actual day in and day out of it, but our goals are the same. He's willing to wait through it."

"There is absolutely no alternative, so that makes it difficult," Mark said. "We're always limited to a few days at best, and it always seems that even in those few days there's hardly any time or something goes wrong. However, this method is healthier than any other. I don't believe in anything else."

Colleen added, "If you're going to be a Catholic, you have to live as a Catholic. You can't pick and choose: 'I like this, but I don't like that.' I'm not going to stand in front of Jesus trying to account for myself, knowing that I've done something that I'm not supposed to do."

"The benefit of Natural Family Planning is that you're doing the right thing," Mark said. "You're open to life. You're following the teachings of the church."

"I think it helps that we agree on that," Colleen said. "We're not at odds over the basic question, although it may be challenging from time to time. We made sure we agreed on the big things before we married."

# CHAPTER THIRTEEN

# What Is Just Cause?

*Michael and Lauri Hahn*

When Lauri and Michael Hahn married, they found themselves in a position shared by many young newlywed Catholics: going to Mass but unconcerned about teachings of the church, not ready to have children and on the birth control pill.

"I wasn't interested in what the church had to say," Lauri said. "I didn't know the teaching. If you weren't ready for kids right away, you went on the pill, and that was that."

"Lauri already had made up her mind, and I never pushed the issue," Michael added. "I only said, 'If you want to have kids, we can have kids.' It was not an issue for me, so I just went along with it. I was an accomplice."

Michael was one of six children. His father helped form his attitude toward when and how many children to have. "He made a couple of comments that I have never forgotten," Michael said. "One thing he addressed was the financial aspect of family life. My father is an accountant, and he budgeted the family finances to the penny. We always had enough to eat, and we were always able to do what we had to do. But he said, 'If you wait until you can afford kids, you will never have them.'

"So I never had the financial concern. If you have the

will, you can figure out how to provide for the family needs. My experience proves this."

When Lauri was ready to have children, she stopped taking the pill. Eighteen months later she and Michael were parents. Their daughter Marie brought about a change in their thinking toward the church and the regulation of births.

"When you have your children baptized, you promise to bring them up in the faith," Michael said. "And at that moment I had a spiritual encounter. I thought, 'What am I promising here? What exactly am I saying?'" Michael said.

"My faith was always there, but it wasn't an explicit part of my life. When I was growing up, being Catholic was something you did. You went to church. But with my daughter's baptism I started to grow in my faith."

Lauri and Michael gradually learned more about the faith and about the church's teaching regarding birth control. "We didn't use any contraception between our first and second children," Lauri said. Matthew was born twenty-seven months after Marie's arrival. Then Lauri obtained a pamphlet on Natural Family Planning and called a local hospital to sign up for an NFP class. Since then the couple has been using the method.

"In the process there was quite a bit of confusion on my part as to when and why to use the method," Lauri said. "I learned that NFP was not supposed to be used as a birth control method. NFP is only for people with a 'just cause' to control the size of their family. I have a problem determining what 'just cause' means. There is no definite yes or no concerning just cause. You have to figure it out for yourself.

"I felt as though I shouldn't even use Natural Family Planning because I was using it as a birth control method.

Part of me was saying that I shouldn't have control; this is God's plan. Whatever I receive from him I should just accept.

"But my third child, Thomas, was difficult to care for when he was an infant. This awakened me to the meaning of 'just cause.'" Adding to the cause was a work project Michael had that required him to travel to Mexico, leaving Lauri at home with three little ones.

"Once the Mexico project was finished, I stopped traveling," Michael said. "October of that year, 2002, would mark our tenth anniversary. So in August we left the children with relatives and took a seven-day cruise to Bermuda.

"This vacation, coupled with the facts that Thomas was older and that I was no longer traveling, helped us to settle down again as a family. Using NFP, we planned for a summer baby. Shortly after our cruise Lauri became pregnant with our fourth child, and Therese Rose was born in June 2003.

"Therese was such a happy, docile baby and toddler that perhaps we grew a little complacent in our use of NFP. Joseph Michael, our fifth, was a surprise." Joseph was born in March 2005.

"We are currently using NFP to avoid pregnancy because Joey is quite young," Lauri said. "At this point we are both slightly apprehensive about having another child. However, past experience tells us that this may change. God will guide us."

Lauri and Michael had not discussed their family planning when they were first married. "It is an uncomfortable subject when you are still getting to know your husband," Lauri said. "I shied away from it. But once we started with the method, we learned that it takes two to discuss it and decide what to do."

"I feel one of the biggest benefits of NFP has been the impact on our relationship, because the conversation alone opens us up," Michael agreed. "It becomes a conduit to a better relationship. We learned about each other's fears and feelings, more so than when it was assumed that she would just take a pill every day and not think about it again.

"It makes us consider all the different things we should take into account before making a decision on whether or not to have another baby. There are important things to consider. For example, we held off with our third because I felt that my second child needed a little time to mature."

Lauri added, "The spiritual growth that I have had these past few years and the stronger relationship with Mike have convinced me that Natural Family Planning is one of the best things we could have done for our marriage."

# CHAPTER FOURTEEN

# The Feminist Mistake

*Matthew and Mary Wenke*

Matthew Wenke learned while working at a pharmacy that hormonal contraception could have an adverse effect on a woman's health and that it could cause the abortion of a newly conceived baby. He decided he could never ask the woman he married to use the pill.

In high school Mary Wenke saw a chart that taught her that all of the hormonal contraceptive choices available had side effects. She decided she wouldn't shoulder that risk for any man.

Sounds like a match, even though it took them a while to find each other. He was thirty-two when they married, and she was twenty-eight. Fourteen years and five children later, their convictions and their marriage remain strong.

"A hormone is a foreign chemical that women take to make themselves available for sex whenever it's wanted, certainly to avoid pregnancy. But seeing the side effects of the pill and learning about that, I wondered why any woman would want to ingest a foreign substance for this purpose when there are other choices," Matthew said. "I wondered how a man could expect a woman to ingest the pill and not feel some sense of responsibility for the side effects that she might be experiencing."

"My mother was active in pro-life work, so I knew there was a connection between abortion and contraception,"

Mary said. "There's a continuum in the mentality of not respecting life or the gift of life, whether it's by contracepting or aborting."

Mary and Matt didn't learn NFP until after the birth of their first child and two miscarriages. With doctors urging them to wait five or six months before attempting to have their second baby, they started to be formally trained in NFP. They have used it over the years to avoid and to achieve pregnancy.

"We had four children born within five and a half years," Matt said. "After our fourth child, we were overwhelmed and just couldn't imagine having a fifth. This was in August or September of 1999, when our youngest was a little less than a year old. We prayed about that.

"At Christmas time I had a dream of a child knocking at our door. In the dream I wouldn't answer the door. I don't know why; I just wanted to pretend that we weren't home. I let the knocking go on.

"I said to myself in the dream, 'Why am I doing this? That little girl really wants to come here, and I'm pretending I'm not home.' I felt this was dishonest, and I really did want to see the child. I ran to the door, and she was already headed to the neighbors'. There the dream ended.

"The next morning was Christmas Eve, and at lunch I shared the dream with Mary. 'What do you think that means?' I asked. She said, 'I think you know very well what that means. Maybe it's the answer to our prayers.'

"We both felt very sure that God was telling us that we ought to have another child. And we wanted another child. Without the openness NFP promotes, that discussion never would have happened. Our fifth child, whom we love dearly, wouldn't have come about. He's a really great blessing to us."

"People look at us and say, 'It doesn't work, obviously; look at all your kids!' That is not true," Mary said. "In fact, when we started the method, we were asked how many children we wanted, and we said five or six. We wanted a large family. To us this is a blessing, not a curse."

"Recently we felt overwhelmed again," Matt said. "Our baby is five years old now. We're not feeling ready just yet, but we're not ruling out having another child."

"Each month we have to talk about our level of openness," Mary added. "If you are sterilized or are contracepting, the possibility of being open to another child is rarely if ever broached. When times are rough or your kids are driving you crazy or you're not financially where you want to be, you say, 'We're not going to have any more children,' and that's the end of the discussion for the rest of your marriage.

"People even ask us now, 'Are you done?' I don't know. Right now I can say yes, this month we're not trying to conceive, but we don't know what's down the road.

"Because we can talk about something this personal so easily, it helps us communicate in other areas of our marriage. We talk about very intimate things on a regular basis. We are very close."

Matt agreed. "NFP has helped make our sex life more a matter of mutual decision. We discuss this every month. As a mental health counselor I see a lot of couples who don't discuss sex at all. There isn't the open, ongoing communication that we have to have if we're going to use this method.

"When we started using NFP, it was very frustrating to

not have intercourse as often as I would have liked. I had to continually focus on why I was doing this. But over time I developed self-control, and now I see benefits to the method that I wasn't able to see then.

"Our intimate time together is very precious. Because intercourse isn't there all the time, there's always an excitement in our relationship. If it isn't a time when we can have intercourse, then we have tea together, or visit together or work on the normal communication part of our relationship. Periodic, predictable abstinence improves our relationship and our sex life.

"I think couples who are contracepting can find that sex becomes humdrum or a matter of course. They lose sight of what a precious and important thing sexual intimacy is. With NFP I don't take our intimate time together for granted."

"A relationship based only on sexual intimacy loses the emotional connection," said Mary. "We are dedicated to building the strong emotional bonds necessary to keep our marriage alive and flourishing. We read novels out loud to each other. We look for ways to communicate to each other and to connect with each other, other intimacies besides sexual intimacies. We don't watch TV. I believe that this strong emotional connection in turn builds desire and excitement in our sexual intimacy. So NFP is not only about family planning; it is about building strong marriages."

Matt feels that since NFP requires that both spouses bear the burden of family planning, practicing it keeps their marriage in balance. "The feminist movement and our secular society have inserted contraception into our culture as the answer. But if I were taking a pill that could have side effects for me, and she wasn't taking anything, then there'd be resentment there. If anything, contraception exploits women by telling them they have to be available all the time. It promotes a negative view of the blessing of children. In counseling I have asked women who consider themselves feminists, 'Have you considered that the new countercultural movement for Natural Family Planning is a feminist thing?' It could be a very positive thing for the feminist movement. But women say, 'No, I'm not going to put myself at risk.' They look at me as if I'm from some other planet when I frame NFP this way."

"I think part of the reason for the church's teaching is its respect for women," Mary said. "I can imagine women rolling their eyes at this statement. But I believe that contraceptive use sets women up for trouble. It's abusive to women. Society has tricked women, in the name of women's rights and sexual freedom, into believing it's for our own benefit. But is it really? Who really benefits?"

# CHAPTER FIFTEEN

# Living Our Vocation
# as Parents

*David and Michelle Marciniak*

David Marciniak's vocation discernment was quite a trip. He thought he had a call to the priesthood and entered the seminary. Some priests and prayer there quickly showed him he was mistaken. So he left and married Michelle.

After the birth of their first child, the Marciniaks experienced a crisis of faith and became Easter-Christmas Christians. Eventually they discerned their true vocation in life: husband and wife with children. People along the way helped direct them, but it was Natural Family Planning that brought them to an understanding of their vocation.

The seed of discontent early in their marriage had been planted years earlier in their religious instruction, which Dave called "coloring pictures of the Holy Family, discussing our feelings and self-actualizing.

"There wasn't anything that was teaching us about the faith. So we both went through this real period of disillusionment with the church and weren't even sure we were meant to be Catholic. We started looking at other churches, trying to figure out where we fit in."

"We didn't really know and understand what our faith taught; that was our biggest problem," Michelle said. "What did it matter? You can be Catholic, you can be

Protestant. I didn't even understand what Eucharist meant, who I was receiving, even after years of going to Communion."

At their pre-Cana classes they told their instructors they wanted two or three children. Natural Family Planning did get a brief mention.

"They handed us a pamphlet," Michelle said.

"And we put it in the circular file," Dave reported.

A colicky daughter in their first year of marriage made them consider again the number of children they wanted. "We couldn't understand why anyone would want more than one after her. We spent most of our nights driving around in the car just to get her to go to sleep," Michelle said.

"We were not going to church," Dave said. "Maybe for religious holidays, that was about it. Michelle was using the pill. We had decided that was the best thing for our family."

"We knew the church taught that artificial birth control was wrong, but I always thought the unspoken secret was that it was OK," Michelle said. "It was no big deal. Yeah, yeah, the church teaches that, but it's really OK if you use contraception."

As their daughter Emily went from colicky nightmare to angelic one-year-old, the Marciniaks changed their minds about having a second child. Michelle stopped taking the pill, and a second daughter, Elizabeth, was conceived.

At this time the first life-changing person entered their lives. A deacon who worked with Dave turned them on to Cursillo.

"Cursillo encourages you to look at your faith like a tripod," Dave said. "The first aspect is piety, and that is your relationship with Jesus Christ. The second is study, and that is looking at religious works, the signs of the times even, and forming your faith. It is learning about the church and about God's will in your life. The third is action, bringing Jesus into the environments you find yourself in.

"Cursillo made Michelle and me realize how poor our formation was. We realized we were just infants in the faith. It inspired this desire in our hearts to be good Catholics.

"And we had heard that good Catholics didn't use contraception. So we stopped using contraception, found ourselves a Natural Family Planning teacher and started learning about it."

"We were rubbing elbows with all kinds of people in Cursillo, so we had some really good influences in our lives," Michelle added. "People were inspiring us, and we really wanted to become good Catholics. We started NFP with that in mind. That was the first change for me in my way of thinking.

"I also desired to become a really good mother and a really good wife. It was more than just something to do in life; it was my vocation.

"It took a few years for me to come to this point. I was a social worker, and I had a really good job. I made more money than Dave did. But it became more important to me to stay home and take care of my children. This was our life; this was who I was."

Michelle quit her job. One week later she found out she was pregnant with their third child, Tyler.

One thing the Marciniaks lacked in their formation was the reasoning behind why contraception is not a licit method of family planning but NFP is. "We were on shaky ground as to why we were using Natural Family Planning," Michelle said. "Our thought was, 'We've got three now, maybe we should go back to using the pill.'"

And so they did. Then they encountered a second life-changing person.

"We went to the pro-life chain on Niagara Falls Boulevard here in Buffalo, New York," Michelle said. "We had the three kids in the car. We were driving down the street trying to find a spot where we could stand. We were looking at the people with all their signs, and there was one guy who had a humongous sign."

"It was non-regulation," Dave added.

"It was pointing out that the birth control pill aborts so many millions of babies a year," Michelle continued. "I started crying because I had taken my first pill that morning. I said to Dave, 'Do you really think that's true?'"

Dave was not caring about what the sign said. He was mad because the guy had a sign that was not the same size as everybody else's and said something different. Everyone was supposed to be holding an "Abortion Kills" sign.

"But I got Dave's attention. He saw me crying, and I said, 'Do you think that's true?' This was before he was a nurse, so he said, 'I don't know.'

"We went home and opened up the long instructions you get inside your pill packet, which we had never read. We finally realized the side effects it could cause, after I had been on the pill for years."

"Most importantly we realized that you could have a baby in the womb and have it aborted by using these chemicals," Dave said. "We had never realized that before.

It certainly wasn't explained to us by the OB/GYN or by anyone.

"That was why that man was standing there with that sign. We never knew who he was, and we never saw that sign again. I wish I could have, because that was a pivotal moment in our lives.

"We had just begun to consider ourselves pro-life. As we looked at these little children we had, we decided that we were indeed pro-life. That was what God wanted for us as we went through our holiness formation. Through evangelization we realized indeed God's will in all of our lives to be pro-life. The pills went into the garbage immediately, and we never looked back."

The Marciniaks began studying why they were making these decisions. They realized they had true vocations, "that it wasn't just priests and nuns who had vocations, but husbands and wives," Michelle stated. "We started thinking and praying about the fact that our marriage was a sacrament, and through that sacrament we could receive graces. All we had to do was ask.

"That would help us on the bad days, when the kids were driving us nuts. The next thing you know, along comes Number Four."

"I think Natural Family Planning gave us an intense love for life that we didn't have before," Dave said. "We realized that Natural Family Planning was going to be an aid for us to have children. It was a way for us to bring life into our home the way we saw our vocation was calling us to do. That was God's will in our life. We were to be a family in a big sense."

The Marciniaks became just that. After seventeen years

of marriage, they have nine children, from infant to high school age!

They found an outlet for their vocation through involvement with St. Luke's Mission of Mercy. This is a center and residence for the needy on Buffalo's east side, located in a former church. The people it serves are primarily from broken homes or broken relationships.

"We find that we are an example and a source of strength for these people," Michelle said. "Often they find comfort in being with us. This ministry has been a big role for our family.

"NFP has given us a big appreciation of life and love for life." It also helped them realize that "if the church was right about this, then the church could be right about anything.

"You can't get much more personal than Natural Family Planning," Michelle explained. "If Jesus is a part of sex in the bedroom and a part of the way the family on a very elemental level develops, then Jesus needs to be a part of everything. That was a great eye-opener for both of us. Every aspect of our lives became enmeshed with Jesus and our being Catholic.

"It's become who we are. People feel comfortable with a large family. When we have people for dinner, you'd think they would run away in horror because it's so loud. The grown-ups eat last so we can be sure everybody has their food. People get into it. They grab a kid and say, 'OK, John Paul, what would you like?'

"This is real family life. I used to get upset when it wasn't neat, but not anymore. The bottom line for me, when we sit at the dinner table and have food sitting here and thank God that no one ever goes hungry in our house, is 'Who would I have not sitting here? Who would I give up?' Not a single one of them. Each is a unique gift to me. Using Natural Family Planning is a gift to me."

The Marciniaks joke about the stability NFP has given their marriage. "When you have nine kids, you're not going to leave," Dave said as his face lights up. "She says, 'You work in a hospital with all those pretty nurses.' And I say, 'They look at me and say, "Nine kids, what a catch."'"

The biggest catch for the Marciniaks is that when they allowed Jesus into their bedroom, he became the Lord of their house.

"So many things followed after that," Michelle said. "I go to daily Mass. I have to depend on God. Jesus is the center of our lives because we can't do it alone—not just money-wise but to keep ourselves going. There are those days when I've yelled at the kids for the millionth time and I think, 'What am I doing?' NFP made him the center of our lives, the center of our marriage, someone we can go to when we are mad with each other.

"Natural Family Planning was the start of looking at our lives and at our marriage and what we were going to be. Our marriage has been a vocation for us, and not just an option that you pick."

"Better late than never," Dave added.

# THE LEAP
# OF FAITH

## How NFP Helps Couples
## Develop Trust in God

Nearly all of the Natural Family Planning couples we interviewed mentioned that faith was an element of their daily lives. This doesn't mean that NFP cannot help couples who lack faith. However, practicing NFP can help a couple discover and grow in faith.

Practicing NFP in marriage removes one barrier to faith: contraception. Lionel Tiger writes: "The pill emancipated women and placed into question existing moral and religious systems that focused on controlling sexual behavior."[1]

Catholic couples who practice NFP aren't forced to question their faith when the topic of contraception is raised at Mass. Many sources support the fact that going to church is a factor in marital success. The Heritage

Foundation, a conservative think tank that publishes research on domestic, economic, foreign and defense policy, combined studies on the benefits of church attendance and found it a primary factor in marital stability. Couples who attend church frequently were found to be 2.6 times as likely to have intact marriages, compared to couples who attend less than once a year.[2]

Couples using NFP often go on a spiritual walk together. They see in the complex workings of their fertility the beautiful plan designed into our nature. They find that when they live in accordance with that nature rather than fighting against it, they can experience God through their marital union.

Lionel Tiger said one of the casualties of the 1960s was trust in institutions and trust in people to act in certain ways. This lack of trust has infiltrated the institution of marriage, where couples surrounded by divorce no longer trust that they will stay together to take care of each other "till death do them part."

"Our social system seems quite unable to persuade or even coerce young men and women to unite in productive and reproductive couples," Tiger wrote. "Another new feature of the system affects men powerfully: Daughters must now be raised to be able to take care of themselves. The divorce rate and the number of people living alone make this a necessity."[3]

Natural Family Planning requires a great deal of trust between spouses. The husband must trust that his wife is diligently making accurate observations and properly charting, and she must trust that when he assents to intercourse during a fertile time, he will fulfill all the commitments that fatherhood entails.

The couple also develops trust in God. They trust that he knows what is best for them. Living the NFP lifestyle shows that a couple has this trust, that they are willing to let Jesus Christ into the most intimate aspect of their lives and to let God's will be done. They realize that they shouldn't tamper with the way God created them.

This surrender can have a powerful effect on both the couple and society at large. As the *Navarre Bible* says in its commentary on Romans 1:24–32: "Every time man knowingly and willingly tries to marginalize God, that religious aberration leads to moral disorder not only in the individual but also in society."[4]

Cooperating with the natural order can help us eliminate the impurity that fouls our daily lives. "Blessed are the pure in heart, for they shall see God" (Matthew 5:8). Surrendering is hard because it goes against our disordered desires, but those who do it present a powerful witness to others. It is an action that speaks much louder than words.

CHAPTER SIXTEEN

# Message Received!

*Steve and Mary Schumer*

Steve and Mary Schumer had two children when they began practicing Natural Family Planning. Following their faith was the motive behind their switch to NFP. Very difficult pregnancies were the motive to limit their family to two children.

"We decided that contraception was not how we should be living our lives. We wanted instead to follow the church's teachings," Mary said.

As a nurse practitioner, Mary found it easy to understand the scientific basis of NFP. So she and Steve jumped right into it. "It's been wonderful," she said. "I think it's brought us closer together in our marriage because sex is something we need to talk about."

"Stopping birth control removed a burden from our shoulders. It's been liberating," Steve added.

Mary found the same thing true in her professional life. "A couple of years ago I was working in a pro-choice private practice," she said. "One of the doctors was involved in abortion, but I separated myself from that part of the practice. I thought I was doing that, anyway, because I never referred patients to him. But I was fooling myself. Even after Steve and I started using Natural Family Planning, I was prescribing birth control pills and diaphragms."

Mary attended a retreat with Father Corapi, where he called the medical profession to task. "'If you profess to be Catholic,' he said, 'you have to live as a Catholic and you have to practice as a Catholic.' As he said these words, he turned to where I was sitting and looked directly at me. And I thought, 'OK, this is something that I really have to look at.'

"I had been feeling that prescribing birth control was not right, even though I kept saying to myself, 'Well, we're not using it ourselves!' I was still prescribing, and I knew I was guilty of leading people astray."

Shortly after the retreat Mary was saying the rosary during eucharistic adoration. In the middle of the sorrowful mysteries, "All of a sudden I felt myself in a crowd of people. It was almost as if I was transported from before the Blessed Sacrament and could see everyone around me. And they were all partying and jeering and shouting.

"I looked through the people, and down the hill I saw Jesus Christ carrying his cross toward me. I realized the people were shouting and jeering at him. He stopped directly in front of me. He turned and looked directly at me, into my eyes. I looked back, and I heard myself saying, 'I can't; it's my job.' Jesus turned away from me and continued up the hill.

"Then I was back in the chapel, kneeling before the Blessed Sacrament. All I could think was 'Message received.' Just the feeling of his turning away from me scared me half to death."

Mary went home and told Steve what had happened. "This is it," she told him. "This is the time."

It was difficult leaving the nice job with salary and

benefits that Mary had held for eleven years, but it was a good thing. She now works for the Catholic Health System.

"My patient load has changed. I worked in an upscale private practice, where I saw people with private insurance. Now I'm working with a clinic population, with people who are uninsured or underinsured. And I love it. Some patients from the private practice have actually followed me to the clinic, which is very nice."

When Mary made this switch, she also started teaching Natural Family Planning. "It was time for payback. I had spent all those years prescribing artificial methods, and I felt it was time I started educating people in natural methods. We've been very blessed with that."

The blessings have spilled into other things the Shumers do. They give the sex talk at the parish pre-Cana classes, much to the relief of the other instructors. They have been able to guide many couples to the truth of the church's teaching.

Steve said, "I tell the husbands-to-be in marriage prep, 'This is not a cup of tea, but neither is the rest of your life. Good things come to those who wait, and guess what, tonight's not the night.'

"*Abstain* is not a word that fits easily into my vocabulary. I never actually use the word; I'll usually describe it in another way. I might say guy-to-guy, 'Some nights you can't.' That's a different way of saying the same thing."

"Then you find other ways to express affection," his wife added.

"Absolutely. You can give her a back rub instead and go to bed," volunteered Steve.

"I think a lot of people are into instant gratification. And that's a problem," Mary added. "We've been taught that you don't have to wait for anything. But sometimes it's good to wait. One of the couples in marriage prep said, 'It's kind of like Lent, when you've given up candy. How good does that chocolate bunny taste on Easter morning?' That's a good way to look at it."

In her work Mary has also advised couples on how to use NFP to achieve pregnancy. One couple had a three-year infertility history. They started using NFP and were pregnant within two months. "It was all in the timing," Mary said. No one had ever discussed NFP with this couple before.

"People are really focused on their bodies: how to keep your cholesterol down, how to increase your brain power, how to control your weight," Steve said. "But this is one bodily mechanism for which people just assume you use medicine, when it's really not necessary."

Mary also began working with ProjecTruth, a character-based, abstinence-only program that's been implemented in schools. "I get to work with teens, which is one of the positives," she said. "It's pathetic what's happening to our teen population. Some medical people find it so easy to give them birth control pills and not address the issue of sex. People don't want to tell these kids that there's a different way to do things. It is scary. Teens learn about other things. They should learn about this too.

"The rate of STDs has never been higher. It's amazing how many different types of STDs young people come in with. We now know that 90-plus percent of all cervical cancers come from human papilloma virus.

"It's been wonderful hitting all these middle schools, high schools and clinics where my colleagues and I can talk to teens. We've also started going to colleges, bringing fertility awareness along to teach these young women about their bodies and how they work. It's like a precursor to marriage, where they can learn how to take care of themselves. Then, when it comes to that point where they are thinking about family planning, they can go back and say, 'I know how this works.'

"We also have a men's-only night to teach boys all about this. We're hoping to start bringing it to other places."

The Schumers are grateful for the message they received from the Lord, and they haven't kept it to themselves.

# CHAPTER SEVENTEEN

# Living Our Faith

*Gary and Michelle Dorobiala*

How you live your life can be a powerful witness to other people. Gary and Michelle Dorobiala had been married less than four years when their second child was born in the summer of 2005, but their use of Natural Family Planning already has allowed them to evangelize at work and in pre-Cana instruction.

Michelle heard about Natural Family Planning on a Catholic radio station when she was engaged. She knew this would be a perfect fit for her and her fiancé, because neither of them wanted to use birth control.

"I knew this was the right thing to do. My parents always said that when you are husband and wife, you have to be open to having children, and if you're using artificial contraception, you're saying 'No' to God. When we're using NFP, we're always open to the fact that, if it's God's will, then we will have children. And we will see them as blessings, not as mistakes."

Michelle told Gary about NFP, and they started studying the Creighton Model during their engagement. "I'm glad we went to the classes beforehand," Michelle said. "This isn't something that you want to try to learn right after getting married."

"This seemed to be not the only choice but the best choice, not only for our faith but also for our relationship and for Michelle's health," Gary added. He and Michelle brought the NFP discussion to the pre-Cana classes.

"We met a fun young couple the first night," Michelle said, "and we hung out with them the first two classes. Then the organizers asked us to speak about what we were learning about NFP. People were surprised. When we said we would avoid pregnancy by abstaining, someone shouted, 'Holy cow!' It was funny.

"The couple we'd met said that they were interested, so we gave them the number to call and encouraged them to go to the initial workshop, the introduction. So we have converted one couple."

The Dorobialas used NFP to avoid pregnancy in the first year of their marriage, in order to get to know each other better. "We were charting before we were married, so we were comfortable with it," Gary said. "I was a bit skeptical at first, but after the success we've had I'm a lot more confident. The quality of our relationship, I would have to say, is just great. I feel that we're closer than most couples that we're friends with because of it. There isn't anything we can't discuss."

He and Michelle continue to find many opportunities to speak to other people about NFP. "I can be very honest and open with people I know," Michelle said. "If somebody asks and they're truly interested, I won't hesitate to tell them about it.

"I've been teaching at my school for many years, so I feel very comfortable talking to young people," Michelle said in an interview six months after they were married. "Many of them have children already, so we always talk about children and things like that. Of course, if you feel comfortable with a group of young girls, they're going to ask you, 'What form of birth control are you going to use?'

"When I said, 'Natural Family Planning,' they said, 'What! Are you nuts?! It's the rhythm method.'

"They couldn't differentiate between the two methods. And once I told them that I have a book on NFP, that it's scientifically sound and 98 percent effective, and that there's research out there and classes at the hospital, they were very intrigued.

"One of the former teachers, who's now on child leave, called me to find out, 'Any kids yet?' They had a pool at work for when I would get pregnant, waiting for me to 'make a mistake.'

"Nobody won any pools because we didn't slip," Gary said. "All our pregnancies were planned."

Gary is also a schoolteacher. The proof of their planning is the fact that both of their children were born in the summer, when they were not working. Michelle miscarried her first pregnancy.

"There are different ways to approach NFP with my colleagues," she said. "One of the things I tell them is that it not only opens the lines of communication with your spouse but also is more beneficial for you physically, especially if you have any health problems. If you take the pill you can get blood clots, develop cancer or have fertility problems. People seem to want to listen."

Michelle married late and was thirty-seven when her second child was born. This is not an unusual scenario for teachers, who often postpone a first pregnancy in order to get established at their schools and then earn a master's degree to hold on to their positions.

"When they decide to have children it is harder," Michelle said of women who put off starting families. "This method is helpful. When others are trying to get pregnant, people using NFP aren't winging it."

Michelle appreciates the opportunity to live her faith in her work environment. "A majority of the people I work with are Catholic, and they have lots of questions, not just about NFP," Michelle said. "Because they know that we have embraced NFP, our faith is obvious. I have a prayer basket at home, and on a daily basis people come up to me and say, 'Would you mind putting so and so on your prayer list?'

"I've copied novenas for fellow teachers and slipped them into their mailboxes. They know they're from me, and they come and thank me. So little by little a pocket of believers is developing. A few of them have gone back to church."

God has blessed the Dorobiala family, and he is blessing many other people through their witness.

# CHAPTER EIGHTEEN

# Walking the Walk While Giving the Talk

*Gregg and Colleen Larkin*

Colleen and Gregg Larkin went to their pre-Cana sessions with questions. Colleen wanted to know about birth control, and Gregg wanted to learn how to share in his fiancée's faith. They didn't get their answers, but they did get a lot out of the classes.

"I wanted to know why the Catholic church was against contraception," Colleen said. "The speakers were great, but they were our parents' age, so to them NFP was the rhythm method. They had no real answer for me."

"They weren't prepared for that question," Gregg stated.

"One of the other topics was faith," he added. "I was a lapsed Catholic and wanted to become an active Catholic. I didn't want to be one of the people who just show up at church on Sunday and put money in the basket. I wanted to get more involved, to take an active role in the Mass. Colleen had faithfully attended Mass every week, and it was important to her that we go together."

So they did, joining the parish choir. Still the question of contraception bothered Colleen, who was on the pill to control irregular periods and wanted to get off so she could learn what was going on with her body. And Gregg still wanted to learn more about his faith. God found a way to fulfill both their needs.

The choir director was also the leader of the pre-Cana program. When the Larkins mentioned how much they liked their marriage-prep class, they predictably were recruited to speak to the next group of engaged couples. At their first pre-Cana meeting as a sponsor couple, they heard a speaker from the diocese give a very direct talk about Natural Family Planning.

"It was amazing," Gregg said. "She was vibrant and bouncy and kept people's attention, getting right in people's faces and challenging them. It was a very fun talk, but it also sparked something in Colleen. She already had a desire to get away from using the pill. She turned to me and said, 'Hon, I'm really interested in this. Let's go and find out more about it.'"

"Three days before this whole thing happened, I had made the decision that I wanted to get off the pill," Colleen confirmed. "I was starting to get freaked out about being on it for a long time, afraid that when we wanted to get pregnant we'd have trouble. I knew of people having that problem."

The diocesan speaker refuted everything Colleen had grown up believing about Natural Family Planning. "Everything I had heard of prior to this was about the rhythm method. I had been told my cycles were too irregular and I'd have all kinds of problems avoiding pregnancy or achieving it. Not true.

"NFP was physically what I needed, so we explored the option together. Things took off from there. God listens when you speak, and if you're open, he answers back. This method is body, mind and soul."

The Larkins became so enamored with NFP that they gave witness talks throughout the diocese. Practicing it in their marriage and learning more about it to enhance their talks helped them blossom spiritually.

"It pushed me to understand more about my faith," Colleen said. "Up until that point I had taken for granted that the church was wrong with regard to the teachings on contraception. All of a sudden it was as if a light clicked on, and I realized, 'Wait a second, here's something that I have been close-minded about, but it makes sense. Maybe there are other things I'm wrong about too.'"

"When we first started using the method, we just focused on the science of it," Gregg said. "Then, as we got more involved, we kind of grew into the spirituality of it."

"I think it's put more focus on our wanting Christ in our lives," Colleen said. "Faith is something that has taken more of the driver's seat in our marriage than I thought it would when we married thirteen years ago. We went up to the altar, and we pledged to each other and to God that we would take each other for better or for worse. NFP helped kick the awareness of our vows—not only to each other but also to God—into high gear. Until you take away 'the safety net' of contraception, you don't realize how much more fulfilling your marriage can be."

The next step on Colleen's spiritual journey involved children. On her thirtieth birthday she was thinking about whether or not she wanted to be a mom. She admits to being scared about having kids, feeling that she had little maternal instinct.

"The answer came surprisingly in the form of my husband's twin nephews," Colleen said. "His sister and her then four-year-old boys were coming up for a week, and I was absolutely, positively terrified about having these kids here. How were we going to handle these little guys?

"The first day didn't look too good. We had to consider moving the cats to another location because the children were petrified of animals. I thought, 'This is our house, the cats live here, you adjust.'

"As the week went by, I became accustomed to having Mark and Ryan around the house. It was really pleasant having these two little boys greeting us every morning with hugs and kisses before we went to work and later when we walked back in the door.

"The morning they left, the house felt quiet and empty. It had never felt that way before, and it was a deafening silence. It made me realize how empty my life would be without children.

"I think God heard what I was feeling in my heart, because this was also the morning that Reilley was conceived. God just hears me when I have these fears. He answers those questions. He saw the opportunity and seized the moment.

"The effectiveness of this method is wonderful, but what we'd learned really came into play while I was pregnant. I was able to look at things from a whole different perspective than many pregnant women who I hear whining all the time, 'Oh, God, I'm so pregnant, I'm so miserable, I'm so tired. I can't wait for this to be over.'

"Oh, I had my moments during my pregnancy, but even then I felt that we were co-creators with God. Had I not been using NFP, I wouldn't have felt that way. I would have been bemoaning the morning sickness and exhaustion more than I did.

"I felt really wonderful about both of my pregnancies. I

felt so full of life, even when my hip joints just burned with Reilley, even when I had gestational diabetes for the last part of my pregnancy with Jack and had to be at the hospital half a day every other day. Having that feeling of life made pregnancy pleasurable."

The question in the Larkin household became baby number three. Gregg, as he approaches forty, is worried about getting his kids through college before he retires, as well as paying for it, since they went from two incomes to one.

"If we do have a third child, we need to talk about a car payment," he said.

"I am not driving a mini-van," his wife insisted.

"If it wasn't for teaching about NFP, particularly teaching the faith portion of NFP, we wouldn't have a basis for this conversation," Gregg said. "NFP has given us great opportunities for some great conversations. It's a journey."

"It's a journey that we're doing together," said Colleen. "NFP helped open our minds to a lot of things that we may have just dismissed. We heard someone speak to our minds that night in 1992. We've been listening to God speak to our hearts ever since."

# CHAPTER NINETEEN

# Letting God Into All Areas of Our Life

*Daryl and Lynda Hostetler*

Daryl and Lynda Hostetler say their story is more about faith in God and Jesus Christ than about Natural Family Planning. But their faith is the reason they practice NFP. Their story is about the abundant way in which God rewarded their faith.

"Lynda was raised Catholic, and I was not," Daryl said. "Even though the use of artificial means of birth control is acceptable within most Christian churches, it never seemed to make too much sense to me. I thought that the Catholic church's approach made more sense."

"I think NFP goes according to God's will," Lynda said. "I can't say that about artificial means of birth control."

"If you have faith in God, you put your trust in him for all aspects of your life," Daryl added. "That would include the fact that he can take care of your needs financially. You should not try to do things on your own and decide that you want exactly a certain number of children during a certain period of time. That's playing the role of God. That takes away from the faith that he might have a different idea."

The Hostetlers' faith led them to use NFP from the start of their marriage. It has been a huge blessing.

"We decided we would wait about two years before trying to have children but would accept their coming earlier," Lynda said. "So we started trying to achieve a pregnancy in November of 1999. We went several months with no success. That's when we started to think that there might be a problem, because we knew that Natural Family Planning is highly accurate."

"Not only in avoiding pregnancy but in achieving pregnancy," Daryl said.

Statistics bear this out. Within the first month of trying to achieve pregnancy using NFP, about 75 percent of couples with normal fertility succeed. Within three months the success rate is 90 percent. If a woman is not pregnant after six months, there most likely is a problem. [5]

Throughout the previous two years Lynda had been having recurring episodes of intense abdominal pain. One doctor called it appendicitis; another diagnosed a urinary tract infection. One morning Lynda went to the emergency room. A subsequent sonogram at her OB/GYN's office showed a large ovarian cyst. Surgery revealed a severe case of endometriosis as well as ovarian cysts. The doctors removed portions of each ovary, leaving her with a lot of scar tissue.

An NFP doctor gave Lynda a 50-50 chance of being able to get pregnant after the surgery. The resident assisting the doctor thought her chances were much less.

"I didn't let that get to me," Lynda said. "I took it to mean that it was either God's will we have children or it was not. We were coming to terms with the fact that we might not have children, but we always held out hope that we would."

Two weeks later, on a visit to the eucharistic adoration chapel at her parish, God showed Lynda five places in Scripture where women who were considered barren had children. "After that experience I felt comforted and optimistic that I would have children," Lynda said.

The doctor told Daryl that Lynda would have to go on medication for three months after the surgery. Afterward they could try again. The condition could come back as soon as six months later, so the doctor advised the couple not to wait long.

"We started trying right away, and again Natural Family Planning came into play," Lynda said. "If you have a short window of time in which it is possible to achieve a pregnancy, you want to be pretty sure you know what you are doing. I wouldn't want to be at that point of uncertainty—about whether or not I could get pregnant and how much time I had to get pregnant—and be playing a guessing game.

"Women tell me all kinds of crazy means to determine whether or not they are ovulating. It's nice to know that there is a scientific method that actually works, and that if we use it correctly we will get pregnant. Since we could determine well the day I was ovulating, we knew that if we didn't get pregnant it was because I wasn't fertile."

Lynda was able to get pregnant their second month of trying. Their son Arik is four years old. Again the doctor advised the couple not to wait if they wanted another child, as repeated infertile cycles would cause buildup of the endometrium, perhaps necessitating further surgery.

"We knew we wanted to have more than one child, so we didn't wait very long." Lynda said. Sadly she miscarried, but she soon became pregnant again. Their second son, Adam, was born in 2004. They also were able to conceive a third child, due in April 2006.

"You may have a lot of faith in certain areas of your life,

and in other areas you want to hold back and try to have control yourself," Daryl said. "With NFP you acknowledge that God's will for sexual intimacy is not a sort of selfish interaction between you and your spouse.

"He created sex for man and woman, and he wanted it to be for your pleasure but also for procreation. The two purposes can't be separated. Natural Family Planning allows us to understand how they go together."

# AFTERWORD

# Marriage Insurance

*Rev. Richard M. Hogan, NFP Outreach*

At a marriage preparation program, the speaker, a priest, suggested to the couples at the beginning session that they invest in some "marriage insurance." He said that this insurance policy would not cost them a dime. It would cost them only time and effort.

Father explained that the teachings of the church regarding marriage and familial love were a kind of marriage insurance. If couples were to follow the church in their marriage, the risk of divorce would almost disappear.

How can the church, especially the spokesmen of the church—a group of celibate older men—know anything about marriage? The answer is that God invited Adam and Eve to marry and to populate the earth. God established marriage at the dawn of creation, and so marriage is a theological question that can only be answered by knowing something about God. The church knows something about God.

Marriage was not an "add on" to creation. It is not an afterthought of God. God created Adam and Eve; "male and female he created them" (Genesis 1:27). God created us as masculine and feminine persons so that we could fulfill ourselves as images of God. Of all the earthly beings God created, only human beings are created in his image and likeness. Therefore we are called to do what he does.

What does God do? God loves. Love is *the* act of God. We are called to love as God loves. As persons with bodies, we are called to express that love in and through our bodies, our flesh and blood. Such a vocation, inscribed in our very being, would have been impossible without the differences between the masculine and feminine—without God's creating us male and female.

Further, as images of God, we cannot truly know ourselves or know how we should act unless we know who God is and how God acts. Our Lord Jesus Christ, the incarnate Second Person of the Trinity, reveals God. He said to Philip, "He who has seen me has seen the Father" (John 14:9). Therefore, in the words of the Second Vatican Council, Jesus Christ reveals "man to man himself."[1]

In other words, as images of God, human beings find out who God is and how God acts in and through Christ. Christ reveals God, and in revealing God he reveals who we are and how we should act. He reveals what it means to be an image of God. Thus the Lord reveals man (what it means to be a human being and how a human being should act) to man (each of us individually).

This is the gospel of the Lord. The church teaches this gospel. Therefore the church continues the work of Christ in revealing man to man himself. And she reveals who we each are and how we should act. The church knows about love and marriage because Christ's gospel reveals love and reveals the way God loves.

## The Body: God's Gift

In listening to the gospel of Christ, taught by the church, couples have a program that will help them live their married life. It is a kind of marriage insurance against divorce.

Sadly, many couples in our culture do not want the insurance policy. As a result, divorce has risen dramatically. How do you live a marriage when you do not know what marriage is or how it should be lived? This is precisely what a majority of couples are trying to do. They may have a glimmer or two of what they are doing, but it sure would be easier if they had the full truth, the full reality, of marriage.

The gospel is challenging, but marriage is hard too if the couple does not know what love is or how to do it. Fundamentally, the rejection of the gospel is the reason our society is in crisis. The family is the basic cell of society. "The future of humanity passes by way of the family," Pope John Paul II said.[2] When marriage is in difficulty, so is all of society.

What is the revelation of Christ? What is this "marriage insurance"?

It is impossible to go into all its details here, but one aspect of the gospel as it pertains to marriage is the teaching against contraception. Every form of contraception alters or harms a healthy, major, functioning system of the human body—namely, human fertility. The human body is part and parcel of the gift of life. Our parents cooperated with God in giving us life. God created us as persons with bodies so that we could manifest and express what it means to be a person in and through our bodies.

The creation of human persons was the last note in the symphony of creation. On the sixth day God created human beings—persons with bodies. This act of God could not have been foreseen, because the only other persons in the universe were the three Persons in God—Father, Son and Holy Spirit—and the angels. None of them have bodies.

God created other parts of the universe—the heavenly bodies, the animals and plants—before he created Adam and Eve. The animals and plants were living bodied beings, but they were not persons. After God created these earthly inhabitants, he found them "good" (see Genesis 1:21, 25). On the sixth day he created the first human beings, the first persons with bodies, and then "God saw everything that he had made, and behold, it was *very good*" (Genesis 1:31, italics mine).

We are the treasures of God's earthly creation because we are persons with bodies. We are like the three Persons in God and the angels in that we are persons; we are unlike them because we have bodies. We are like the animals and plants in that we are living bodied beings, but we are unlike them in that we are persons. We are a mixture of person and body, an enfleshed spirit, a spiritualized body.

Why would God create such an odd entity as the human being? The late John Paul II, in his Theology of the Body addresses, gave us the answer: We are created as images of God with bodies to express and manifest person-hood in and through our bodies.

The body, the pope teaches, speaks a language, the language of personhood. We are the only beings in the universe who can manifest or express what it means to be a person in a visible way. We express ourselves in and through our bodies, and when we act as we should—that is, like God—we not only express our own persons but actually manifest God himself. We make visible what has been hidden in God—who is a communion of three Persons—for all eternity. Only we, as embodied persons, can do this.

Our bodies are sacred and holy. They participate in the dignity and value we all possess as images of God. They express and manifest divine realities. How else could Jesus reveal the Father in his body? If the human body were incapable of revealing divine truths, how could Christ's body have been the medium for the revelation of the Father—that is, for the gospel?

## Confronting a Contraceptive Culture

This is not the view of the body found in our culture. There the body is often viewed as a kind of machine, something to be owned and operated. The cry of the extreme abortionist lobby is "It is *my* body," meaning "I own it" and "I operate it."

If the culture is right, the "one flesh" union of the spouses in the marital embrace is impossible. If their bodies are just machines, their union would not be interpersonal at all. It would be two machines touching, something akin to computers linked together via the Internet or through a server!

The only view that married couples can accept is the one the church proposes: the body is sacred. It is the expression of ourselves and even of God.

It follows necessarily that contraception is terribly wrong. If the body is the expression of the person, and if the body speaks the language of personhood, it does so through its healthy biological functions. The body is more than the sum of its biological parts. It is through the apparently understandable biological functions that the mystery of human personhood is expressed. To alter or harm a healthy, major, functioning aspect of the human body is to attack and harm the language of the body. Contraception attacks the body, and what is done to the body is done to the person.

Contraception is also wrong because it attacks married love. Marriage is a union of love between a man and a woman (both images of God). As images of God, all human beings are called to love as God loves, and this is particularly true of marriage. When God loves, it is always and in every case life-giving. Our love too must be life-giving.

Contraception alters the marital embrace, as the spouses close off the possibility of life. This harms marital love because the couple denies themselves the opportunity to love as God loves.

For these reasons the message of the gospel, the message of the church to all married people is *don't do it*. This is the "marriage insurance" that the priest at the engaged program was proposing that the couples buy.

## NFP: Life-Giving and Love-Giving

The alternative to contraception is Natural Family Planning. NFP actually is a "reading" of the language of the body. Those who study human fertility through NFP read the body's language of love. They come to understand that the body is the expression of the person and even of the divine Persons.

This knowledge leads to a respect and awe of the

human body and person. The married person comes to respect himself or herself and the other, the spouse. There is wonderment at the gift the other is, and this wonderment leads to generous love.

Further, NFP respects the loving marital embrace. It allows couples to love as they should, with an openness to life. As Pope Paul VI expressed it in *Humanae Vitae*, each and every marital act in an NFP marriage is "open to the transmission of life."[3] NFP builds marriages because it leads the couple to read and understand the bodily language of love and because it builds love in the marriage.

The stories of the couples in this book are a living testament to the success of the gospel as "marriage insurance." Try it; you'll like it—because it will strengthen your marriage.

Is it difficult? Of course. What is worthwhile is often difficult. But it is not impossible. You have access to the help of God and his church through the sacraments and grace.

# CONCLUSION

# Not Catholic
# Birth Control!

The purpose of this book is to help Christians live a sacramental marriage. The couples interviewed testify to the many graces that have come into their lives through the natural regulation of their family size, in conformity with the age-old teaching of the Catholic church. They bear witness to the profound ways in which Natural Family Planning goes beyond birth control, and they show how the sharing of love and fertility is an irreplaceable gift of marriage.

Many Catholics wonder if there is any difference between NFP and contraception. It is true that people can use it with a contraceptive mentality. Modern methods of NFP are so effective that some opponents say that couples who use it are not trusting God to determine the size of their family. Such an objection, valid as it is, overlooks two basic facts of Catholic teaching on birth regulation.

First, nowhere does the church teach that couples must trust their family size to blind faith. *Humanae Vitae* acknowledges that couples can use reason along with faith to determine the size of the family God calls them to have. The only stipulation is "that husband and wife recognize fully their own duties toward God, toward themselves, toward the family and toward society, in a correct hierarchy of values."[1]

Second, Natural Family Planning, unlike contraception, maintains the vital link between the love of the spouses and their openness to life. NFP does nothing to change the nature of the physical act of love in marriage, and therefore it preserves marital love in the form designed by God. This tends to keep couples mindful of the connection between their sexual love for each other and the children who are the natural result of this love. This ongoing "mindfulness" that NFP instills often leads couples to be generous with life, even while using a morally licit method of "planning" births.

Further, we must bear in mind the interior changes that the practice of NFP brings to most people. John Paul II alluded to these changes in a December 7, 1996, address to those attending a course for natural methods of fertility regulation, sponsored by the Catholic University of the Sacred Heart.

> The scientific validity of the methods and their educational effectiveness makes them increasingly appreciated for the human values that they presuppose and strengthen....
> Their humanizing character is all the more obvious from the fact that using the natural methods requires and strengthens the harmony of the married couple, it helps and confirms the rediscovery of the marvelous gift of parenthood, it involves respect for nature and demands the responsibility of the individuals. According to many authoritative opinions, they also foster more completely that human ecology which is

the harmony between the demands of nature and personal behavior.

At the global level this choice supports the process of freedom and emancipation of women and peoples from unjust family planning programs which bring in their sad wake the various forms of contraception, abortion and sterilization. [2]

The Holy Father then threw his support behind those attempting to spread knowledge of these methods.

"The Church is grateful to those who, with personal sacrifice and often unacknowledged dedication, devote themselves to the study and spread of these methods, as well as to the promotion of education in the moral values which they presuppose.".... The moment has come for every parish and every structure of consultation and assistance to the family and to the defense of life to have personnel available who can teach married couples how to use the natural methods. For this reason I particularly recommend that Bishops, parish priests and those responsible for pastoral care welcome and promote this valuable service.[3]

Following are a few citations from the *Catechism of the Catholic Church* about the purpose of sex within marriage and about the regulation of birth.

The spouses' union achieves the twofold end of marriage: the good of the spouses themselves and the transmission of life. These two meanings or values of marriage cannot be separated without altering the couple's spiritual life and compromising the goods of marriage and the future of the family. (CCC, #2363)

Fecundity is a gift, an *end of marriage*, for conjugal love naturally tends to be fruitful.... So the Church, which is "on the side of life," teaches that "it is necessary that each and every marriage act remain ordered *per se* to the procreation of

human life." "This particular doctrine…is based on the insep-
arable connection, established by God, which man on his own
initiative may not break, between the unitive significance and
the procreative significance which are both inherent to the
marriage act." (*CCC*, #2366)[4]

Periodic continence, that is, the methods of birth regulation based on self-observation and the use of infertile periods,
is in conformity with the objective criteria of morality. These
methods respect the bodies of the spouses, encourage tender-
ness between them, and favor the education of an authentic
freedom. In contrast, "every action which, whether in antici-
pation of the conjugal act, or in its accomplishment, or in the
development of its natural consequences, proposes, whether
as an end or as a means, to render procreation impossible," is
intrinsically evil. (*CCC*, #2370)[5]

## Opinions Based on Fact

While there is not universal agreement in the scientific
community about the effectiveness of NFP, its positive
effects in marriage or the side effects of hormone-based
contraceptives, an Internet search of media, medical and
government sites provided backing for the claims made in
this book.

The effectiveness ratings for NFP vary widely depend-
ing on the source. Studies by the World Health
Organization and the U.S. Department of Health and
Human Services report 97 to 98 percent effectiveness when
NFP is learned from a certified instructor and practiced to
the letter.[6]

The actual user effectiveness rating from these sources
is 85 to 95 percent. Couples need to be really committed to
NFP in order for it to be effective. They often err in the
three days after a woman's peak signs of fertility have been
observed. An NFP instructor will say that a couple *is* trying

to conceive a child if they have intercourse on a day of fertility, regardless of stated intentions.

As to the issue of marital stability, the U.S. Census Bureau reported that divorce increased from 2.5 per thousand to 5.0 per thousand married couples from 1965 to 1976.[7] The Centers for Disease Control and Prevention released a report in 2001 that stated that 43 percent of first marriages end in separation or divorce within fifteen years. These numbers were based on the Survey of Family Growth results for women fifteen through forty-four years of age, taken in 1995.[8]

Studies on divorce among NFP users are hard to find. John Kippley, who with his wife Sheila heads the Couple to Couple League, cites an informal survey that put the figure at less than 1 percent. The Couple to Couple League's survey of a small group of NFP users found a divorce rate of 1.3 percent. Kippley admits, "Since this was a special, dedicated group, we estimate that the rate for the general population of NFP users might be higher, perhaps even two or three times that rate.... On the basis of the information we have, we think a 5% divorce rate among couples practicing NFP is really the outside maximum limit."[9]

Using one number from a study is like pulling one verse out of Scripture to prove a point. This is probably the case in statistics showing the low divorce rate among practitioners of NFP. There are many factors that go into a successful marriage. This study has focused on one, albeit an important one.

A couple learning a method of family planning that requires periodic abstinence may worry that if they want to avoid having a child, there won't be any time available for sex. Let me point out that situations such as the couple's in chapter twelve are atypical. With practice and prayer, most couples are able to determine fertile times and enjoy a satisfying sex life. Many will say that the quality of their times together more than makes up for the times of abstinence. As Rick Karnath states in chapter seven, "This gift is worth waiting for."

The U. S. Conference of Catholic Bishops cites a study on its Web site that shows that couples between twenty-five and thirty-four years of age have intercourse nine times per month, and couples eighteen to twenty-four and thirty-five to forty-four have intercourse eight times a month.[10] If a couple abstains during menstruation and during the woman's fertile period, they will have fourteen to sixteen days in a twenty-eight-day cycle in which to make love. This gives them plenty of time for intimacy. There is a drawback in that to avoid pregnancy they will have to abstain when the woman's libido is highest, which is during her fertile period.

In the introduction we stated that most Protestants, even those who are decidedly pro-life, do not agree with the Catholic church in its teachings on contraception. Yet the Worlings and the Hostetlers attest to the fact that there are Protestants who are coming to see NFP's advantages. Two books written by Protestants that promote the use of NFP are *Birth Control for Christians: Making Wise Choices* by Jennell Williams Paris (Baker, 2003) and *Open Embrace: A Protestant Couple Rethinks Contraception* by Sam and Bethany Torode (Eerdmans, 2002).

### A Look at the Pill

The witness couples also made claims about the effects of hormone-based contraceptives on a woman's health and

on the life of a newly conceived child. These claims, especially those linking the pill and breast cancer, are in dispute
among scientists, and this is not the forum for attempting
to settle the debate. Yet here are a few things to think about.

Joel Brind, professor of endocrinology at Baruch
College of the City University of New York, and Dr. Angela
Lanfranchi, a breast surgeon and member of the Expert
Advisory Panel for the New Jersey Board of Examiners,
wrote a booklet for the Breast Cancer Prevention Institute
titled "Breast Cancer: Risks and Prevention." Among the
factors that increase breast cancer risk are

- an induced abortion, especially when the termination
  occurs before the first full-term pregnancy, when it is
  late-term or when the woman is in her teens
- use of oral contraception, particularly when use is prolonged and before the first full-term pregnancy
- prolonged use of hormone replacement therapy
- first pregnancy occurring at a later age
- never having breast-fed
- never having had a full-term pregnancy[11]

Dr. Chris Kahlenborn, author of *Breast Cancer: Its Link to
Abortion and the Birth Control Pill*, reports on his Polycarp
Research Institute Web site that, as of 2003, twenty of
twenty-three retrospective studies show that women who
take oral contraceptives prior to their first full-term pregnancy also have an increased risk of developing breast
cancer.[12]

Women who develop breast cancer tend to have more
estrogen in their systems than women without breast

cancer. One-third to two-thirds of all breast tumors have estrogen receptors and depend on estrogen for growth. Estrogen stimulates cell division, which can cause mutations of breast cancer genes to multiply and become permanent. These genes can be passed from mother to daughter.

Most oral contraceptives contain estrogen. In Dr. Kahlenborn's research, the increased risk of breast cancer among women who used the pill persisted in the ten years after the use of the pill was stopped.[13]

The International Agency for Research on Cancer (IARC), an arm of the World Health Organization, conducted a study of women infected with the common sexually transmitted human papilloma virus (HPV), a cause of most cervical cancers. The study noted a higher risk of developing the cancer in women who had taken birth control pills for more than five years. Women who had taken the pill for ten years or more were four times more likely to get the disease than those who had never taken it.[14]

The American Cancer Society predicted at the start of 2005 that 10,370 women would get invasive cervical cancer in the United States that year. While early detection has caused deaths from cervical cancer to decline significantly, about 3,710 women were expected to die from it in 2005. [15]

## Other Contraceptive Risks

The worst side effects of the pill, such as stroke, occur in very small percentages. But with 11.6 million women on oral contraceptives in the United States in 2002, a small rate still puts tens of thousands of women at risk.

Researcher Dr. John E. Nestler and his colleagues from Virginia Commonwealth University and Université de

Sherbrooke in Quebec, Canada, said that the risk of having a heart attack or stroke is twice as high for women who take low-dose oral contraceptives than for those who don't. The report, released in the summer of 2005, said the risk returns to normal when pill use ceases.[16]

Further study links other contraceptives to health risks. The Associated Press, in a story released July 16, 2005, said women using the birth control patch had nearly triple the chance of dying or suffering a survivable blood clot than women using the pill, which itself increases the chance of a clot. Using Food and Drug Administration records, the AP reported that "about a dozen" women died in 2004—out of 800,000 users—from clots believed to be related to the patch.[17]

Pfizer Canada, Inc., in consultation with Health Canada, released information on June 30, 2005, on the risks of bone loss associated with the birth control shot Depo-Provera:

> The data indicate that women who use Depo-Provera may lose significant bone mineral density. The longer Depo-Provera is used, the more bone mineral density may be lost. Bone mineral density may not return completely once use of Depo-Provera has been discontinued. This is of particular concern when Depo-Provera is used in adolescence...when bone mineral density should instead be increasing.[18]

## Risks to the Family

Of particular concern to pro-life couples is the risk of unknowingly aborting a child. Certified fertility instructor Katie Singer cites studies that show that the progestin-only pill "may not suppress ovulation or conception from occurring." When conception does occur, the pill disrupts the passage of the embryo through the fallopian tubes and prevents implantation in the uterus, which amounts to an early abortion.[19] Dr. Paul Weckenbrock, reporting for the Couple to Couple League, said that ovulation occurs in two percent to ten percent of cycles of women taking the pill.[20]

Drs. Walter L. Larimore and Joseph B. Stanford reviewed available evidence that oral contraceptives could block a fertilized egg—what they called a pre-embryo— from attaching to the endometrial lining of the uterus. They found that there was insufficient data to determine how often oral contraceptives cause such abortions. However, they did say that breakthrough ovulation—and the risk of fertilization—is more likely with pills with lower doses of estrogen.

Evaluations of women for at least six cycles "demonstrated ovulation rates ranging from 1.7% to 28.6% per cycle. For progestin-only pills, reported breakthrough ovulation rates range from 33% to 65%." In their conclusion they said available evidence "supports the hypothesis that when ovulation and fertilization occur in women taking OCs [oral contraceptives], postfertilization effects are operative on occasion to prevent clinically recognized pregnancy."[21] In other words, the young embryo is aborted.

Using contraception to delay having children until couples are established in their careers also has its negative effects. According to the Centers for Disease Control and Prevention (CDC), older women are more likely to use fertility drugs to get pregnant, and such drugs often lead to multiple births, which carry a higher risk of premature labor and low birth weight. The Associated Press reported on February 11, 2004, that in the United States infant mor-

NOT CATHOLIC BIRTH CONTROL!

tality climbed in 2002 for the first time in more than four decades, in part because of older women putting off motherhood. Recent birth rates for women ages thirty-five to forty-four were the highest levels for those age groups in three decades, the CDC reported.[22]

## Hope for Marriage

The great strength of NFP is that it requires a spouse to focus on what's best for the other and not on his or her own wants. And spouses do this in the most intimate aspect of their married lives. They acknowledge that life may not go as planned, and they pledge to stand by each other regardless of circumstances. This embodies " 'til death do us part."

A group called Divorce Reform polled lawyers for the leading causes of divorce. The top five were poor communication, financial problems, a lack of commitment to the marriage, a dramatic change in priorities and infidelity. There are other factors that separate people, such as addictions, ill health and physical abuse.[23]

Natural Family Planning certainly can't claim to be a cure-all for the problems that plague couples. However, many couples attest to the fact that NFP promotes communication, commitment, mutual respect, faith in God and sexual compatibility. When it comes to a successful marriage, that's a pretty good place to start.

# Resource Guide

Information on Natural Family Planning may be hard to find at both the parish and diocesan levels. Here is a list of providers who can give you accurate information on it and on how you can start learning one of the methods.

Web sites for the Billings Ovulation Method:

http://www.woomb.org

http://www.billingsmethod.com

http://www.boma-usa.org

http://www.naturalfamilyplanning.ca

One More Soul keeps a national list of NFP providers and practitioners. It also serves as a great resource for anyone with questions about contraception and natural methods of fertility regulation.

One More Soul
1646 N. Main Street
Dayton, OH 45405-3832
800-307-7685
www.omsoul.com

The Pope Paul VI Institute for Human Reproduction researches natural methods of fertility regulation and trains doctors and practitioners in these methods. The Institute also seeks to treat women's health problems—such as those for which oral contraceptives commonly are prescribed—in ways that aren't hostile to life.

Pope Paul VI Institute
6901 Mercy Road
Omaha, NE 68106-2604
402-390-6600
www.popepaulvi.com

The Pope Paul VI Institute teaches the Creighton Model of Natural Family Planning. For more information on this method and to find a practitioner in your area, visit www.creightonmodel.com.

Marquette University is also conducting research into natural methods at its Institute for NFP, 414-288-3854, www.marquette.edu/nursing/nfp/.

Northwest Family Services works with youth, couples and families throughout the United States to educate about and support healthy decisions aimed at building self-respect, forming long-term goals, avoiding drugs and alcohol and understanding the power of sexuality.

Northwest Family Services, Inc.
4805 N.E. Glisan Street
Portland, OR 97213
503-215-6377
nfs@nwfs.org
www.nwfs.org

The Family of the Americas Foundation promotes family unity by encouraging parents to meet their mutual responsibilities to each other and to their children.

Family of the Americas Foundation
P.O. Box 1170
Dunkirk, MD 20754
301-627-3346
family@upbeat.com
www.familyplanning.net

The Couple to Couple League International is a great source of information on the sympto-thermal method and on the pitfalls of contraception.

Couple to Couple League International
P.O. Box 111184
Cincinnati, OH 45211-1184
513-557-2449
www.ccli.org

NFP Outreach uses parish missions to spread the word about NFP.

NFP Outreach
3366 NW Expressway
Building D, Suite 630
Oklahoma City, OK 73112
888-637-6383
www.nfpoutreach.org

The United States Conference of Catholic Bishops provides NFP information at

www.usccb.org/prolife/issues/nfp/index.htm
Call 212-541-3240 or 212-541-3070 for specific questions.

# Glossary

**Abortifacient**: Anything that unnaturally causes the death of an unborn child. This includes hormone-based contraceptives and devices that prevent an egg from implanting in a woman's uterus.

**Achieving**: Sexual behavior that may result in a pregnancy, whether intended or not.

**Avoiding**: Refraining from intercourse during times when a woman is fertile.

**Basal body temperature**: Temperature of the body at rest, usually taken before a woman gets up in the morning. This temperature rises with ovulation.

**Billings Ovulation Method**: An NFP method that teaches women to recognize the fertile phase of their monthly cycle by the presence of mucus and the sensation it causes at the vulva in the days leading up to ovulation. This method was developed by Drs. John and Evelyn Billings and Father Maurice Catarinich of Melbourne, Australia.

**Biomarker**: A visible sign of fertility, such as basal body temperature or cervical mucus.

**Breakthrough ovulation**: Release of an egg while using a chemical means of birth control. Sometimes this egg joins with sperm to become fertilized. It is often sloughed off in the womb as an early abortion because the contraceptive makes the womb hostile to life.

**Cervical mucus**: Fluid generated by a woman's hormones that can guide or block sperm from traveling into the uterus. This mucus changes from opaque and tacky following the menstrual period, to clear and stretchy during the fertile period and then back to opaque and tacky.

**Charting**: The daily written observations of a woman's fertile signs, whether cervical mucus, basal body temperature or both. This charting can include color-coded stickers that correspond to observations. For example, a woman puts a red sticker on the chart for each day of her period, a green sticker when no signs of fertility are present, a white sticker when she is showing signs of fertility and a yellow sticker when non-fertile mucus appears after ovulation.

**Chemical**: For the purposes of this book only, synthetic hormones.

**Clomid**: A chemical, properly named Clomiphene Citrate, that stimulates the ovaries to produce a mature egg.

**Conjugal love**: Love expressed in the sexual union of spouses.

**Contraceptive mentality**: A way of thinking that calls children a burden and a threat to the freedom and happiness of the individual, severs the natural link between creation of life and sexual intercourse and tempts people to abort should intercourse create an "unwanted" life.

**Creighton Model**: A method of determining fertility by examining cervical mucus. It is named after the Creighton University School of Medicine in Omaha, Nebraska, where it was developed. It has grown into a diagnostic tool for women's reproductive health problems.

**Cursillo movement**: A primarily lay movement within the Catholic church that sponsors retreats and other events to equip Catholics with the tools to evangelize by living their daily lives in a fully Christian manner.

**Estrogen**: Hormone that is active in the pre-ovulation stage of a woman's cycle. It stimulates production of luteinizing hormone.

**Eucharistic adoration**: Spending time in prayer with Jesus, whom Catholics believe is present body, blood, soul and divinity in a consecrated Communion host. A host is placed in a holder called a monstrance, which is set in a prominent place in a quiet chapel.

**Fecundity**: Fertility or the ability to have children.

**Fertile period**: The days when a woman observes fertile signs and the chances of her conceiving a child are the greatest. This period runs from the onset of cervical mucus until the fourth evening after peak day. Days of heavy bleeding are also considered to be in the fertile period.

**Follistim**: Trademark follicle stimulating hormone, which encourages the maturation of follicles. It is used by women experiencing anovulation (an absence of ovulation) and by women undergoing assisted reproductive technology procedures.

**hCG**: Chemical that induces follicles matured by injections of Follistim to release eggs.

**Infertile period**: Days when a woman almost certainly cannot conceive.

**Luteinizing hormone**: Hormone that triggers the release of an egg in a woman's cycle.

**Natural Family Planning**: Any of the methods of fertility awareness that allow couples to space the births of their children without interfering with the healthy, natural reproductive functions of the human body.

**Peak day**: The last day before the signs of fertility start to decrease. Fertility signs build until approximately the day a woman ovulates, and then they decrease or disappear. A woman is almost certainly not fertile on the fourth evening after her peak day.

**Polycystic Ovary (or Ovarian) Syndrome (PCOS)**: The most common hormonal reproductive problem in women of childbearing age. Women with PCOS have high levels of male hormones and an irregular or no menstrual cycle. They may have many small cysts (fluid-filled sacs) in their ovaries.

**Post-peak**: The days from peak day until menses. A woman is considered fertile for three full days after the evening of her peak day, even if nonfertile mucus appears.

**Pre-peak**: Days from menses to peak day. In the pre-peak period a woman is considered fertile at the first sign of mucus, even if that mucus lacks the characteristics associated with fertility.

**Progesterone**: The hormone active after ovulation. It prevents further ovulation and thickens the lining of the uterus to prepare it for nurturing an embryo.

**Prometrium**: Natural progesterone, taken orally.

**Sympto-thermal method**: The observation of both cervical mucus and a woman's waking or basal temperature to determine fertility. A third, usually optional, observable sign is the physical change that occurs in a woman's cervix during her monthly cycle.

# Notes

## Introduction: Clearing the Hurdle

1. *CCC*, #2370, quoting Pope Paul VI, *Humanae Vitae*, Encyclical on the Regulation of Birth, July 25, 1968, 12.

2. From an unpublished tabulation from the 2002 National Survey of Family Growth, as provided by William D. Mosher, a statistician from the National Center for Health Statistics. The National Survey of Family Growth (NSFG) is used as a source often in this book because it collects in cycles the largest sampling of what it calls contraceptive practices in the United States. Those numbers are posted by the Department of Health and Human Services on the Web site of the Centers for Disease Control (www.cdc.gov).

3. Teresa Notare, "Ignorance Is Not Bliss," Life Issues Forum, January 4, 1992, available at the U.S. Conference of Catholic Bishops Web site, www.usccb.org.

4. Unpublished tabulation from the 2002 National Survey of Family Growth.

5. Pope John Paul II, general audience, January 16, 1980, www.vatican.va.

6. *Humanae Vitae*, 17. This translation is in the appendix of John Paul II, *The Theology of the Body: Human Love in the Divine Plan* (Boston: Pauline, 1997), p. 434.

7. W. Bradford Wilcox, "The Facts of Life and Marriage: Social Science and the Vindication of Christian Moral Teaching," *Touchstone*, January/February 2005, www.touchstonemag.com.

8. Dr. Robert T. Michael, talk given at Emory University family conference, March 2003, quoted in Wilcox.

9. A 2004 survey conducted by Barna Research Group on U.S. divorce rates. See "Born Again Christians Just As Likely to Divorce As Are Non-Christians," *The Barna Update*, September 8, 2004, www.barna.org.

10. John F. Kippley and Sheila K. Kippley, *The Art of Natural Planning*, 4th ed. (Cincinnati, Ohio: Couple to Couple League, 1996), p. 245.

11. Lionel Tiger, *The Decline of Males* (New York: Golden, 1999), p. 35.

12. Alan Guttmacher Institute, "Induced Abortion in the United States," posted May 18, 2005, at www.agi-usa.org.

13. Stanley K. Henshaw, "Unintended Pregnancy in the United States," *Family Planning Perspectives*, Vol. 30, No. 1, January–February 1998. *Family Planning Perspectives* is published by the Alan Guttmacher Institute, the research arm of Planned Parenthood. The data were taken from three cycles of the National Survey of Family Growth. Visit www.agi-usa.org.

14. *2005 Physicians' Desk Reference* (Montvale, N.J.: Thomson Physician Desk Reference, 2005), p. 3338.

15. All of the medical information is gleaned from four sources: Thomas W. Hilgers, M.D., *The Medical Applications of Natural Family Planning* (Omaha: Pope Paul VI Institute Press, 1992); Thomas W. Hilgers, *The Scientific Foundations of the Ovulation Method* (Omaha: Pope Paul VI Institute Press, 1995); Toni Weschler, *Taking Charge of Your Fertility: The Definitive Guide to Natural Birth Control, Pregnancy Achievement, and Reproductive Health* (New York: Quill, 2002); Katie Singer, *The Garden of Fertility* (New York: Avery, 2004).

16. Weschler, pp. 46-47.

17. Hilgers, *Scientific Foundations of the Ovulation Method*, p. 22.

18. Weschler, p. 53.

19. Hilgers, *Medical Applications*, p. 52.

20. *American Journal of Obstetrics and Gynecology*, October 15, 1981, p. 368, cited in Weschler, p. 350.

21. Weschler, p. 349.

22. Weschler, p. 348.

## Section One: It's Her Body: How Natural Family Planning (NFP) Is Good for a Woman's Reproductive Health

1. Hilgers, *Medical Applications*, p. 140.

2. Weschler, p. 6.

3. Hilgers, *Medical Applications*, p. 69.

4. Hilgers, *Medical Applications*, pp. 97–98.

5. See Shari Rudavsky, "A Pregnancy Breakthrough," *The Miami Herald*, March 11, 2002.

6. *2005 Physicians' Desk Reference*, pp. 3338–3341. This reference is for one brand of oral contraceptive chosen at random. The *2005 Physicians' Desk Reference* lists side effects for each manufacturer's brand of contraceptives.

7. The research of Professor Erik Odeblad, M.D., PH.D. of the Department of Medical Biophysics, University of Umea, Sweden, on the aging of the cervix is available at www.billings-ovulation-method.au. See also Dr. Kevin Hume, "The Biology of the Cervix," at www.woomb.org.

8. Odeblad.

9. Weschler, p. 15.

10. Singer, p. 126.

11. Singer, p. 130.

12. Dr. Stephen Langer, *Solved: The Riddle of Illness* (Lincolnwood, Ill.: Keats, 2000), quoted in Singer, p. 131.

13. *2005 Physicians' Desk Reference*, p. 3339.

## Section Two: Abstinence Makes the Heart Grow Fonder: How NFP Improves the Marital Relationship

1. *Humanae Vitae*, 17, in *The Theology of the Body*, p. 434.

2. Posted on the author's website, http://www.sais-jhu.edu/faculty/fukuyama.

3. Francis Fukuyama, *The Great Disruption: Human Nature and the Reconstitution of the Social Order* (New York: The Free Press, 1999), p. 101. Fukuyama chronicles the societal changes brought by the move from the Industrial Age to the Information Age. These changes, which began in the mid-1950s, were marked by seriously

deteriorating social conditions in most of the industrialized world and by a rapid altering of social values.

4. Fukuyama, p. 102.

5. Tiger, pp. 33–34.

6. Tiger, p. 35.

7. George A. Akerlof, Janet L. Yellen and Michael L. Katz, "An Analysis of Out-of-Wedlock Childbearing in the United States," *Quarterly Journal of Economics*, May 1996, p. 277.

8. George A. Akerlof, "Men without Children," *The Economic Journal*, March 1998, p. 287.

9. Wilcox.

10. Akerlof, "Men without Children."

11. Wilcox.

12. Fukuyama, p. 117.

13. Akerlof, Yellen and Katz.

14. Mother Teresa, "Whatsoever You Do…," address to National Prayer Breakfast, Washington, D.C., February 3, 1994, www.priestsforlife.org.

15. Mother Teresa, statement to the Cairo International Conference on Population and Development, September 9, 1994, www.ewtn.com.

## Section Three: Staying on Course: How NFP Keeps Spouses From Growing Apart

1. Tiger, p. 5

2. Amelia Warren Tyagi, "Why Women Have to Work," *Time*, March 22, 2004, p. 56.

3. Tiger, p. 140.

4. See Keith Naughton, "Three for the Road," *Newsweek,* December 1, 2003, http://msnbc.msn.com.

5. Tiger, p. 143.

6. Jane Aronson compiled figures for 1970 and compared them with 2000 figures for the Puget Sound Center for Teaching, Learning and Technology in Bothell, Washington. She published her findings in a paper titled "Undergraduate and Graduate Status of Women and Minorities in Science, Technology, Engineering and Mathematics," www.pugetsoundcenter.org. *USA Today* reported the 2004 figures on October 20, 2005, in "College Gender Gap Widens: 57% Are Women."

7. Tiger, p. 35.

8. Pope John Paul II, *Familiaris Consortio,* "The Role of the Christian Family in the Modern World," November 22, 1981, 6, www.vatican.va.

9. Fukuyama, p. 10.

10. Tiger, p. 19.

11. Tiger, p. 20.

12. Tiger, p. 54.

13. *CCC,* #2368, quoting Vatican II, *Gaudium et Spes,* Pastoral Constitution on the Church in the Modern World, December 7, 1965, 51, par. 3.

## Section Four: The Leap of Faith: How NFP Helps Couples Develop Trust in God

1. Lionel Tiger, "Nasty Turns in Family Life," *U.S. News and World Report,* July 1, 1996, p. 57.

2. Wesley Shrum, "Religion and Marital Instability: Change in the 1970s?" *Review of Religious Research*, Vol. 21, No. 2, 1980, pp. 135–137, www.heritage.org.

3. Tiger, "Nasty Turns in Family Life."

4. *The Navarre Bible* (Dublin: Four Courts, 1998), p. 74.

5. See Hilgers, *Medical Applications*, p. 52.

## Afterword: Marriage Insurance

1. *Gaudium et Spes*, 22, in Walter M. Abbott, ed., *The Documents of Vatican II*, Joseph Gallagher, trans. (New York: Guild, 1966), p. 220.

2. *Familiaris Consortio*, 86.

3. Pope Paul VI, *Humanae Vitae*, 11, in *The Theology of the Body*, p. 431.

## Conclusion: Not Catholic Birth Control!

1. *Humanae Vitae*, 10, in *The Theology of the Body*, p. 431.

2. John Paul II, "To Teachers of Natural Family Planning," December 7, 1996, 2, as printed in *L'Osservatore Romano*, weekly edition in English, January 22, 1997, and reprinted at www.ewtn.com.

3. John Paul II, "To Teachers of Natural Family Planning," 3, quoting his own encyclical *Evangelium Vitae*, The Gospel of Life, March 25, 1995, 97.

4. *CCC*, #2366, quoting *Familiaris Consortio* 30; *Humanae Vitae*, 11, 12.

5. *CCC*, #2370, quoting *Humanae Vitae*, 14.

6. Notare. See Introduction, note 3.

7. U.S. Census Bureau, *Statistical Abstract of the United States 2003: The National Data Book* (Washington: Department of Commerce, 2004), p. 72.

8. National Survey of Family Growth, 1995, at www.cdc.gov.

9. Kippley, p. 245.

10. "NFP—Myths and Reality," www.usccb.org.

11. Joel Brind and Angela Lanfranchi, "Breast Cancer: Risks and Prevention." This pamphlet can be found online at www.bcpinstitute.org.

12. See www.polycarp.org. Also see Chris Kahlenborn, *Breast Cancer: Its Link to Abortion and the Birth Control Pill* (Dayton: One More Soul, 2000).

13. Cornell University, "Program on Breast Cancer and Environmental Risk Factors in New York," Fact Sheet 10, at www.envirocancer.cornell.edu.

14. See Kristen Finello, "Pill Linked to Cervical Cancer," March 28, 2002, at www.bhg.com.

15. See "How Many Women Get Cancer of the Cervix?" at www.cancer.org.

16. Press release issued by Virginia Commonwealth University, Richmond, Virginia, July 7, 2005. See www.vcu.edu.

17. Martha Mendoza, "AP Finds More Fatalities from Birth Control Patch Than Expected," at www.boston.com/yourlife/health/women.

18. Pfizer Canada, Inc., "New Safety Information on the Use of DEPO-PROVERA Associated with Bone Mineral Density Changes," Kirkland, Quebec, June 30, 2005, at www.hc-sc.gc.ca.

19. Singer, p. 130.

20. See Paul Weckenbrock, R.Ph.D., "The Pill: How Does It Work? Is It Safe?" at the website for Couple to Couple League International, www.ccli.org.

21. Walter L. Larimore, M.D., and Joseph B. Stanford, M.D., MSPH, "Postfertilization Effects of Oral Contraceptives and Their Relationship to Informed Consent," *Archives of Family Medicine*, Vol. 9, No. 2 (February 2000), at http://archfami.ama-assn.org.

22. Associated Press Report, Atlanta, Georgia, February 11, 2004, at www.cnn.com.

23. Americans for Divorce Reform, "What Are the Most Common Causes of Divorce?" at www.divorcereform.org.